ISBN 978-1-9998027-7-6

Halima Publishing
Henley-on-Thames, Oxfordshire U.K.
www.halimapublishing.co.uk

By Yasmin Watson
Original illustrations by Hana Horack-Elyafi

BOOK ONE

ISLAMIC HISTORY

THE MEANING OF JIHAD IN THE LIFE OF THE PROPHET MUHAMMAD ﷺ

SOCIAL CHANGE EDUCATION MILITARY ENLIGHTENMENT

"Gnosis is my capital.

Intellect is the basis of my religion.

Love is my foundation.

Yearning is my mount.

Remembrance of Allah is my intimate companion.

Reliance on Allah is my treasure.

Sorrow is my companion.

Knowledge is my armour.

Patience is my cloak.

Satisfaction is my booty.

Incapacity is my boast.

Doing without is my profession.

Certainty is my food.

Truthfulness is my intercessor.

Obedience is enough for me.

Jihad is my character, and the coolness of my eyes is in the prayer."

The Prophet Muhammad ﷺ (Narrated by 'Ali ibn Abi Talib ر)

Contents

The True Meaning of Jihad

Most of us live in a peaceful society that has taken a great amount of struggle to achieve. There are so many people who continue to work every day to improve things, ensuring everyone has access to food, education, and healthcare.

In countries that have wars, famine or other disasters, it takes a huge effort to bring peace and stability for all.

When the Prophet Muhammad ﷺ was born almost 1500 years ago, life was very hard for many people. There was poverty, slavery, tribal war, oppression, and few rights for women, slaves and children.

Within his lifetime, the Prophet Muhammad ﷺ transformed the whole of Arabian society into one based on the principles of peace and justice for all, regardless of race, gender or social position.

THE PRINCIPLE OF JIHAD

'Jihad' is one of the most misunderstood words of today.

Sometimes it is translated as 'holy war'. This is not exactly correct as 'holy' means something sacred and pure. War is a terrible thing even if it is sometimes necessary, such as in self-defence or to protect society. The term Jihad has a broad meaning and is derived from the Arabic root, *jahada*, meaning "to exert strength and effort, to use all means in order to accomplish a task". So a better translation of Jihad is 'to struggle'. You may have heard the phrase; 'Jihad fi sabilillah'. This means 'to struggle in the way of Allah ﷻ'. That is, to try really hard to please Allah ﷻ with commendable actions, for instance, to try and improve society to make it a just and peaceful one.

A 14th century painting of Ibn Rushd (Averroes) by Andrea di Bonaiuto

1 Jihad of Education and Counsel

The Prophet ﷺ spent thirteen years in the peaceful Jihad of Education and Counsel - patiently talking to the people, guiding them towards good and reminding them to turn away from bad actions, reciting the Qur'an and explaining its meaning. This form of Jihad was never combative in any way and is considered to be one of the greatest forms of Jihad.

THERE ARE FOUR MAIN CATEGORIES OF JIHAD

Scholars since the time of the Prophet ﷺ, such as Ibn Qayyim al-Jawziyyah, Ibn Rushd (also known as Averroes) and modern scholars such as Sheikh Muhammad Hisham Kabbani divide the term Jihad into four main types. Ibn Rushd divided the term further into fourteen different types. The four main groups are: Jihad of the Tongue - *education and counsel*, Jihad of the Hand - *social change*, Jihad of the Heart - *the struggle with the self*, and Jihad of the Sword- *engaging in actual battle*.

In this book, we will explore the noble concept of Jihad - to strive for excellence. This begins with the perfect example of the Holy Prophet Muhammad ﷺ.

> Have you helped a friend with good advice?

How did the Prophet Muhammad ﷺ completely change society over such a short time? What makes him, in many people's estimation, the greatest leader we have ever seen? Why do people today still love and honour him so much?

Jihad of the Hand - Improving Society

2

> How can you help make this world a better place to live?

Do we fight in self-defence? What are the rules of battle in Islam? What is true Jihad? Is there any permission for Jihad of the Sword in these times?

How were the great battles of early Islam fought and what can we learn from them?

Jihad of the Sword - Military and Defence

4

Jihad of the Heart - The Struggle With the Self

3

The Prophet Muhammad ﷺ was sent to perfect the character of people and to guide them to Allah. What does that mean and what is the spiritual journey in Islam?

What Was Arabia Like Before Islam?

What was the world that Muhammad ﷺ was born into like?

Arab warriors were skilled swordsmen and widely feared.

WOMEN WITH NO RIGHTS

Women were in no way equal to men in the eyes of the pre-Islamic Arabs and seemed to have a similar status to horses; admired for their beauty, and bought and sold. They had little or no rights as members of Arab society. There was, however, a great appreciation of feminine beauty - the Arab man falling in love easily as we see in the poetry of the time. When he tired of one, he could go on to marry any number of wives. When he died, his sons inherited the wives (except his own mother).

Baby girls were considered a burden, expensive to feed and clothe with no ability to earn money for a family in the harsh desert, which gave rise to the terrible practice of burying the baby girls alive in the sand.

A noble woman, for instance a daughter of a tribal chieftain, would have had a better position and some authority, but if a woman was not protected by marriage, it was very difficult for her.

MERCHANTS, FARMERS AND SLAVES

The wealthiest among them were the Jews, who had the most businesses, including making weapons. They were also moneylenders, charging very high rates of interest. They would charge 100% interest, so if you borrowed 100 dinars one year, you owed 200 the next year.

Slaves were used all the time, they were bought and sold and treated like animals. They had no rights and formed the most depressed class in Arab society.

Arabs also made money by farming and sending trading caravans to neighbouring areas of Yemen, Persia, Egypt and Syria.

IDOL WORSHIPPING

Most Arabs were idol worshippers, each tribe or clan carried out different practices depending on which idol they worshipped. The various different idols were placed in the Ka'aba along with religious pictures. The most popular idols were Hubal, the goddesses al-Lat, al-Uzza and Manat who were venerated and invoked through a variety of rituals, superstition and divining arrows, as well as ritual sacrifice. People would come from miles around to go for pilgrimage. They would also sometimes go around the Ka'aba in the nude as part of their worship.

OTHER BELIEFS AT THE TIME

There were also the Jews, Christians and the Monotheists. The Monotheists followed the religion of the Prophet Abraham ﷺ Tradition tells that it was Abraham ﷺ and his son Ismael ﷺ who originally built the Ka'aba hundreds of years earlier and since then became an ongoing place of pilgrimage. The Banu Hashim, the Prophet Muhammad's ﷺ clan, were monotheists.

A painting of people worshipping the golden calf, in the time of Moses. Idol worshipping was the main religion of the Arabs. There were elaborate rituals based around a god or goddess linked to a particular statue. People were keen not to anger the idols and gave offerings and prayers.

JUSTICE

Justice was thin on the ground - there was no government, police or courts. The only person of authority was the clan leader. These leaders were able to protect people of their clan, but many were known at the time for their arrogance, conceit and vindictiveness. This often led to horrendous crimes and of course, misjudgements.

If a clan member committed a crime, the clan leader would be obliged to protect that person, but it could result in a tribal feud that lasted for generations. The Arabs actively engaged in war, which to them was an exciting and challenging sport. It was an opportunity to display skills and win honour and glory for themselves and for their tribes.

There were a variety of small towns in the south of Arabia, but most of the people were Bedouins.

Often there was tension between the two, the Bedouins distrusting the townspeople and the townspeople viewing the Bedouins as wild and uncouth, like pirates of the desert.

The most important tribes at that time were the Quraysh in Makkah (Prophet Muhammad ﷺ was Qurayshi) and the tribes of Aws and Khazraj. Noble tribes like the Quraysh had ancestors dating from the Prophet Ismael and were in charge of the Ka'aba.

The Arab Tale Teller by Horace Vernet, 19th century

THE SOFTER SIDE OF THE ARABS - THEIR LOVE OF POETRY

Most Arabs at that time could not read and write but loved to recite poetry and were very proud of their oral tradition. We can find out a lot about Arab culture from studying these poems as the poets were the historians of the era. Here is a poem from Imru'al Qais, one of the most famous poets of that time describing a mountain scene. If a poem was really good, it would be hung in the Ka'aba.

"The mountain, at the first downpour of rain, looked like a giant of our people in a striped cloak....The clouds poured forth their gift on the desert of Ghabeet, till it blossomed...as though a Yemeni merchant was spreading out all the rich clothes from his trunk." Imru'al Qais

Who Was the Prophet Muhammad ﷺ?

Muslims and many others believe that there has not been a man in all of history with greater bravery, wisdom, compassion, and excellent moral character.

How can a man who did not read nor write, one of such kindness and compassion end up commanding and successfully leading armies of hundreds of thousands? Usually, men rise to such power by treachery and force or through climbing the ladder of political hierarchy. He had absolute power in his hands yet was the most humble and kindest of all.

It is these characteristics that continue to inspire such love and devotion over so many years, a man who's grace, generosity and spirituality millions aspire to.

Those who knew him personally gave many accounts of what he was like on a day to day basis so we have a very detailed picture of what he said and did.

The famous poet Imam Busayri ق, wrote these beautiful lines in his famous poem 'Al-Burda' about the Prophet Muhammad ﷺ:

'Abdullah ibn 'Umar ر said: "I have never seen someone who is braver, more generous, more courageous, more radiant or more handsome than the Messenger of Allah ﷺ."

Sayyidina 'Ali ر, the fourth Khalif said: "Anyone who saw him ﷺ suddenly was filled with awe of him. Those who kept his company loved him."

Abu Hurayra ر said: "I never saw anything fairer than the Messenger of Allah ﷺ, it was as though the sun shone from his face."

Ibn Abi Hala ر said: "His ﷺ face shone like the full moon."

"How can people in this world grasp his reality?
They, who are asleep and pleased by dreams from him.
How beautiful what has been said about his reality!
Your light is everything and everything else is particles."

THE NOBLE LINEAGE OF THE PROPHET MUHAMMAD ﷺ

The Prophet ﷺ was born into the noble family of the Quraysh. His father was 'Abdullah ﷜, his grandfather, 'Abdul Muttalib and his mother was Amina ﷜, daughter of Wahab. None of his ancestors ever committed fornication (although this was common in those days) and the Prophet Muhammad's ﷺ ancestral grandfather was Sayyidina Ismael ﷺ the son of Sayyidina Abraham ﷺ and then further back to Sayyidina Noah ﷺ Sayyidina Idris ﷺ, and finally Sayyidina Adam ﷺ.

What Did Allah ﷻ Say About Prophet Muhammad ﷺ?

"We sent you as a witness, a bringer of good news and a warner, one who calls to Allah with His permission and a light giving lamp." (Al-Ahzab 33:46)

"We did not send you except as a mercy to all the worlds." (Al-Anbiya 21:107)

"Those who follow the Messenger, the Unlettered Prophet, whom they find written down in the Torah and the Gospel, commanding them to the right, and forbidding them the wrong, making unlawful for them the foul things, and relieving their burdens and the fetters that are on them. Those who believe in him and aid and help him and follow the light that has been sent down with him — they are the prosperous." (Al-A'raf 7:157)

The Companion Jabir ﷜ said: *"When the Prophet ﷺ went down the road, anyone who followed him knew that he had passed this way because of his scent."*

Umm Ma'bad ﷜ said: *"He ﷺ was sweet in speech, distinct, without using too few or too many words. It was as if his speech was threaded pearls. He had a loud voice, which was very melodious."*

Sayyidatina 'Aisha ﷜ said: *"His ﷺ character was the Qur'an."*

The Companion, Anas ﷜ said: *"I have not smelled amber, musk, or anything more fragrant than the smell of the Messenger of Allah ﷺ"*

The Prophet Muhammad's ﷺ Simple Way of Life

The Prophet Muhammad ﷺ lived a very simple life and had few possessions. So much so, that when his noble Companion Sayyidina 'Umar ر came into his room, he began to cry, and said:

"O Messenger of Allah, how can we allow you to live like this? Look at the Kings of Rome and Persia. Surely O Messenger of Allah, you deserve better?" The Prophet ﷺ replied; 'Is this what we are here for? O 'Umar, are you not happy that they have this world and we have the afterlife?'"

(Sunan Ibn Majah)

The Holy Cloak of the Prophet Muhammad ﷺ at the Topkapi Museum, Turkey.

HOW DID THE PROPHET MUHAMMAD ﷺ SPEND MONEY?

The Holy Prophet ﷺ did not rest until he had given away all his provisions to the poor and needy. He did not store anything until the next day. The Prophet ﷺ said, "I do not feel easy if any gold dinar remains with me overnight, except for a dinar which I have set aside to pay a debt."

He was so generous that people could not match it. When gifts were given to him of gold, jewels and money he would immediately either buy what was needed for the sake of Islam or give it to the poor and needy and put it in the charity fund.

The Prophet ﷺ sometimes would not eat for many days. Even in the time of wealth and prosperity in the later years of Medina, the Prophet ﷺ continued his humble and modest life.

We hear from 'Amr ibn al-Harith ر:

"The Messenger of Allah, ﷺ left only his armour, his mule, and some land which he made as a gift of charity (when he passed to Allah)." (al-Bukhari)

The very pious and high ascetic standard of the Prophet ﷺ was hard to follow; a standard that very few leaders in the history of Islam were able to achieve. Most of the Khalifs in the dynasties that followed, such as the Umayyad, Abbasid and Ottoman, lived in palaces with sumptuous luxuries.

THE HOLY CLOAK OF THE PROPHET MUHAMMAD ﷺ

The Holy Cloak of the Prophet Muhammad ﷺ, made of linen, cotton and silk, was brought to Istanbul during the reign of Ottoman Sultan Ahmad I in the 17th century. Every year during Ramadan, the cloak is put on special display at the Hirka-i Serif Mosque in Istanbul, attracting hundreds of thousands of visitors.

The cloak was first entrusted to Uwais al-Qarani ﺭ, a very pious simple man who went to Medina to see the Prophet Muhammad ﷺ, but had to return to Yemen without seeing him due to his mother's illness.

The Prophet ﷺ then ordered his Companions, 'Umar ﺭ and 'Ali ﺭ to take the cloak and present it as a gift to Uwais al-Qarani ﺭ because of the deep love Uwais had for the Prophet ﷺ, even though he had never met him in person.

The Prophet Muhammad ﷺ wore plain clothes, loose trousers, a coarse outer cloak, and a turban. He preferred wearing white and green. When his clothes wore out, he used to mend them himself. When he was given fine gifts of fancy clothes, he would give them away. He disliked clothes that were for showing off, like fine silks and clothes that dragged on the ground.

The Blessed Sandal of the Holy Prophet ﷺ.

How Did the Prophet ﷺ Live His Life?

The Prophet ﷺ spent most of his time at the mosque, talking with the community and answering their questions. He would also spend time with his family in his home, including helping with the cooking and even mending his own socks. He was often silent, thinking and reflecting about things. Nothing ever angered him except for the sake of Allah.

His time engaged in confict or actual battle was very little, he passed much more time in the daily Jihad of improving society, teaching the religion and spiritually guiding the Muslims.

PRAYER AND SECLUSION

The Prophet ﷺ would sometimes stand for the whole night in prayer, and he slept very little.

One night, his wife 'Aisha ﵃ noticed his feet were swelling up during his prayer. She asked him the next day why he needed to

One of the earliest known manuscripts of the Holy Qur'an written on deerskin.

pray so much as Allah had forgiven all his past and future sins. He ﷺ replied, *"Should I not be a grateful slave of Allah ﷻ?"* *(al-Bukhari and Muslim)*

Another time, one of his Companions arrived at the mosque at night and the Prophet ﷺ was engaged in Tahajjud prayer, the non-obligatory night prayer. The Companion joined the Prophet ﷺ in prayer. The Prophet ﷺ had just begun reciting Surat al-Baqara, the longest chapter in the Qur'an, taking about two hours to recite. The Companion would have been enraptured in the Prophet's ﷺ recitation but it was beginning to feel like a long time

A model of the Prophet's ﷺ Mosque in Medina when it was first built. This can be seen at the Museum of Medina in Medina, Saudi Arabia.

for the Companion, as few could match the devotional strength of the Prophet ﷺ; he assumed that at the end of al-Baqara, the Prophet ﷺ would finish and then go into ruku. Instead, the Prophet ﷺ began the next chapter, Surat Aali Imran, another very lengthy chapter.

The Prophet ﷺ also liked to go into seclusion at different times in his life, and especially in the last ten days of Ramadan.

It was in seclusion when the Prophet ﷺ received the first revelations of the Qur'an. He would then receive revelations from time to time over the next twenty-two years until he passed to the next life.

SPENDING TIME WITH HIS FAMILY

The Prophet ﷺ loved to spend time at home and was an excellent husband and father. When arriving home, he would call out, "How can I be of service?" The Prophet ﷺ would mend his own clothes and help with the chores. He was also playful with his wives and always treated them very kindly.

'Aisha ﺭ, the wife of the Prophet Muhammad ﷺ, was asked, *"What did the Prophet used to do in his house?"* She replied, *"He used to keep himself busy serving his family and when it was the time for prayer he would go."* (al-Bukhari)

LOOKING AFTER THE COMMUNITY AND AFFAIRS OF STATE

The Prophet ﷺ allocated one-third of his time to the people, giving talks, attending to people's needs, visiting the sick and helping the poor.

Al-Husayn ﺭ, the Prophet's ﷺ grandson, asked his father Sayyidina 'Ali ﺭ what the Prophet did in his daily life? He replied:

"He would divide his day into three parts, one for Allah, one for his family and one for his people and himself. He used his time with the people more for the common people than the elite. He would always ask about the people who had asked him things." (al-Bukhari)

This is the imprint of the ring of the Prophet Muhammad ﷺ which he would press into wax to seal official documents.

It says 'Allah's Messenger Muhammad'. The Prophet ﷺ specifically wanted his name underneath the Name of Allah, to show reverence, rather than above it as was usually written; Muhammad, the Messenger of Allah.

A DAY IN THE LIFE OF THE PROPHET MUHAMMAD ﷺ

0:00 – Wakes up for prayers in the home or at the Mosque.

3:00 – Rests.

4:30 – Fajr or dawn prayer at the mosque, gives talks to the congregation.

6:15 – Prays Ishraq (post sunrise) prayer then sees family.

8:00 – Has breakfast or begins fasting for the day.

8:30 – Goes to the mosque for teaching and taking care of social and political matters.

11:00 – Visits relatives and receives guests at home.

12:30 – Prays Zuhur or noon prayer, teaches the Companions and takes care of community issues.

14:00 – Has a short nap

14:30 – Goes out with Companions to help in the community.

16:00 – Prays 'Asr or afternoon prayer in the Mosque.

16:30 – Goes home to spend time with his family.

19:00 – Prays Maghrib or sunset prayer in the mosque.

19:30 – Eats dinner.

20:30 – Prays 'Isha or night Prayer.

21:00 – Returns home to his family.

21:30 – Rests.

Education and Council

Jihad of the Tongue

THE FIRST PHASE OF THE PROPHETIC MISSION

The first phase of the Prophet's ﷺ mission began with reciting the Qur'an to those who followed him, as well as giving spiritual and moral guidance.

The Prophet ﷺ spent thirteen years in this peaceful Jihad, patiently talking to the people, reciting the Qur'an and explaining its meaning. This form of Jihad was never combative in any way and is considered one of the greatest forms of Jihad.

Countless early scholars of Islam (such as Imam Ad-Dardir, Imam Buhuti, Al-Khatib Al-Shirbini) all agree that the Jihad of Education, explaining the religion and removing uncertainties is the essential building block for developing a good and solid faith in a community.

However, there were many people in his home town of Makkah that were not interested in listening and were angry that the Prophet ﷺ told them to stop worshipping idols. Even though everyone in the city believed Muhammad ﷺ to be trustworthy, and all agreed he never lied, they greatly resisted the idea of One God.

When the Prophet ﷺ sometimes became dispirited, Allah ﷻ would send messages of encouragement and hope in the verses of the Qur'an.

In the beginning, the Prophet ﷺ only had a few followers: his wife Khadija ر , his best friend Abu Bakr ر , his young cousin 'Ali ر , and a handful of slaves such as Bilal ر , Zayd ibn Harithah ر and Sumayyah bint Khabbab ر.

The Makkans were very harsh to Muhammad ﷺ, making fun of him and putting him down. The slaves often received life-threatening treatment. Sumayyah ر became the first martyr when Abu Jahl, her owner, found out she was Muslim.

When the Prophet ﷺ heard that his Companion Hadrat Bilal ر was being tortured by his slave owner and struggling to survive under a huge boulder, Muhammad ﷺ told his friend Abu Bakr ﺭ, who then negotiated with Bilal's owner and bought him for a very high price. Abu Bakr ﺭ immediately gave him his freedom. Bilal ﺭ later became known for calling the first call to prayer, the Adhan.

A man asked the Prophet ﷺ what Jihad is best, the Prophet ﷺ said, *"The most excellent Jihad is to say the word of truth in front of a tyrant." (Ahmad)*

The early Muslims were so strong in their faith, that when harshly questioned by the people of Makkah, they would bravely declare their Islam, even if this meant torture or death. This was a very difficult time for the Muslims which they endured with great patience.

WHAT WAS IT LIKE TO HEAR THE PROPHET ﷺ SPEAK?

We hear from Qadi 'Iyad Ibn Musa al-Yahsubi ﺭ who describes him:

"The Prophet's ﷺ eloquence and fluency of speech are well-known. He was fluent, skilful in debate, very concise, clear in expression, lucid, used sound meanings and was free from affectation."

The Prophet ﷺ learnt all the different dialects of the tribes and spoke to them in their own ways. The way he spoke to the Quraysh was very different to how he spoke to the tribes of Najd. Everyone felt heard and understood.

When he spoke, every word could be distinguished, even at the back of the assembly. Those who listened were so still that birds could have settled on their turbans and they would not look up out of awe and respect. He spoke in such a way that was easy to remember.

As well as speaking at the regular prayers, the Prophet ﷺ would also teach in a more informal way. This type of teaching was often about spiritual matters of the heart and explanations of the Qur'an.

Companions of the Prophet ﷺ, both men and women, would pass on to others what they knew of *Fiqh* (Islamic law) and Qur'an after learning from the Prophet ﷺ.

Some sayings of the Prophet Muhammad ﷺ

"Say the truth, even if it is to your detriment."

"When Allah loves someone, He will put him in difficulties."

"Forgive, and Allah will forgive you."

"Allah said, 'O Son of Adam, you will get what you have intended, and you will be with the one whom you love more.'"

"Be in this world as a stranger and a guest, and make the mosques your homes, and teach your heart leniency, and make much remembrance and cry much."

"All Creation is a servant of Allah. The most beloved to Him among them is the one that helps his brothers (or sisters)."

"Make everything easy and don't make it difficult. Give good tidings and don't cause people to run away."

"Be merciful, Allah will be merciful with you."

"Keep Allah and He will keep you. Keep Allah before you. If you need help, ask His Help."

The Holy Qur'an

The Holy Qur'an is central to everything that the Prophet Muhammad ﷺ taught, how he lived his life and how he began to improve society.

The Qur'an itself is organised in a beautiful way, in a version of Arabic that was more perfect than anything the finest poets had ever heard at that time or since.

The Qur'an is considered by Muslims to be Allah's Speech to humankind, and the reciting of it brings healing and guidance to Muslims.

If the Prophet ﷺ did not know an answer to a question, he would wait until Allah revealed the answer in a verse of Qur'an, no matter how long this would take.

The Qur'an contains clear and simple messages as well as being a complex and deep text, which takes years of study from qualified teachers to begin to understand its true meanings.

The Qur'an is also miraculously easy to memorise even though it is composed of approximately eighty thousand words, with children as young as five being able to memorise the entire Qur'an.

THE REVELATION OF THE QUR'AN

The Prophet Muhammad ﷺ did not receive the entire Qur'an all at once. The Angel Jibrael ﷺ brought different surahs on different occasions. The first time was when the Prophet Muhammad ﷺ was in seclusion in the cave of Hira, outside Makkah. As the Angel descended and hugged him, the Qur'an filled the heart of Muhammad ﷺ, which he described as a very powerful and overwhelming experience. He was also informed of his Prophethood on that day. He then went home to his wife Khadija ﺭ, who reassured him and soon became the first Muslim. The first verse begins like this:

"Recite in the name of your Lord who created – Created man from a clinging substance. Recite and your Lord is the Most Generous – Who taught by the Pen – Taught man that which he knew not." (Al-Alaq 96:1-5)

Initially, the Prophet Muhammad ﷺ recited the Qur'an to his Companions who would then memorise the verses. The Prophet ﷺ would also explain the meaning of the verses. Gradually, the verses were written down by those around him and formally gathered together as a complete

Qur'an during the time of Sayyidina 'Uthman ﺭ, as we see here in one of the earliest fragments of the Qur'an, discovered at Birmingham University in the U.K. It is carbon dated between 545 and 645 A.D..

One of the earliest known fragments of the Qur'an

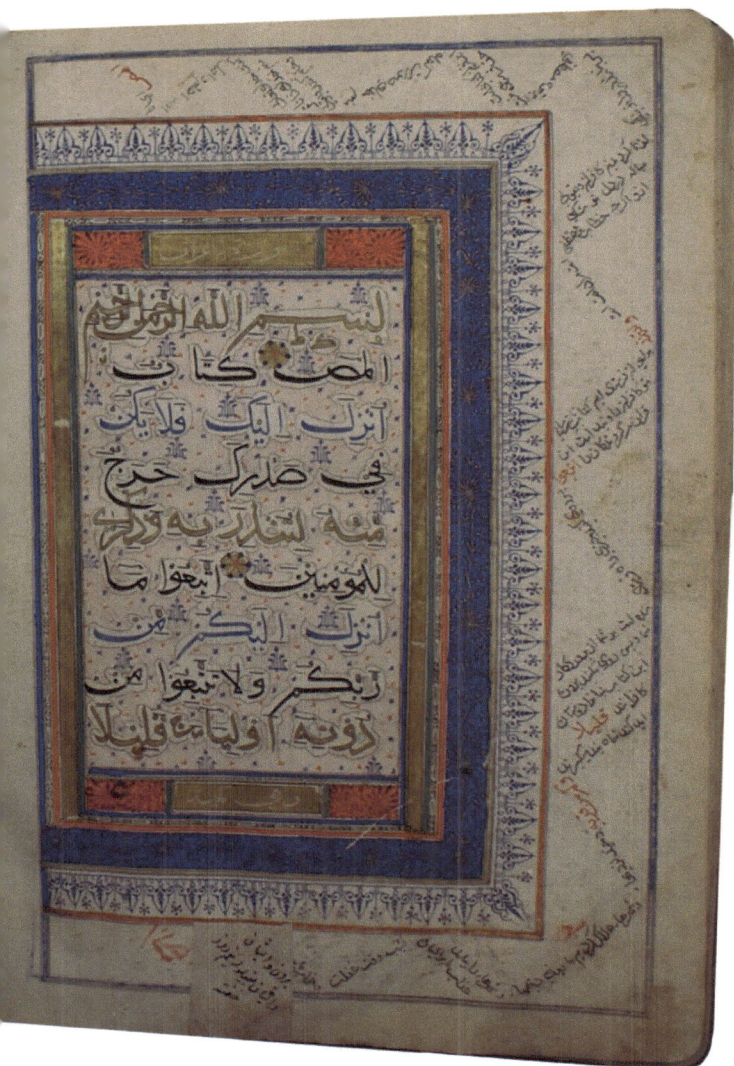

THE ADHAN

The Adhan, or call to prayer, notified the Muslims that the prayer would soon begin.

The Adhan began quite a few years into the Prophet Muhammad's ﷺ mission and after he moved to Medina. The Prophet's ﷺ Companion, Hadrat 'Abdullah ibn Zaid رضي, had a dream where he heard the Adhan, he told the dream to the Prophet ﷺ who confirmed it. The Prophet ﷺ asked the freed slave Companion, Hadrat Bilal رضي, to call out the Adhan because he had such a beautiful voice. This is how the Adhan is recited:

Allahu Akbar
God is Great
(said four times)

Ash-hadu an la ilaha illa Allah
I bear witness that there is no god except the One God.
(said twice)

Ash-hadu anna Muhammadan Rasool Allah
I bear witness that Muhammad is the messenger of God.
(said twice)

Hayya 'ala-s-Salah
Hurry to the prayer (Rise up for prayer)
(said twice)

Hayya 'ala-l-Falah
Hurry to success (Rise up for Salvation)
(said twice)

Allahu Akbar
God is Great
(said twice)

La ilaha illa Allah
There is no god except the One God

For the pre-dawn (Fajr) prayer, the following phrase is inserted after the fifth part above, towards the end:

As-salatu khayrun minan-nawm
Prayer is better than sleep

HOW THE QUR'AN BEGAN TO SHAPE SOCIETY

When the Prophet Muhammad ﷺ migrated to Medina after the conditions in Makkah became life-threatening for the Muslims, a new phase began. Great social change was about to take place. The Prophet ﷺ, as always, was guided by the revelations of the Qur'an and the inspirations he received from Allah in all his actions, bringing about the changes that the society desperately needed.

The Muslims would eagerly wait for Allah ﷻ to send new verses of the Qur'an. Some verses contained new laws and guidance on how to run society. These would be implemented straight away.

The Qur'an began to descend, and like raindrops, the revelations came to sprout goodness on the dry earth. Gradually Arab society transformed until the culture was unrecognisable from its former state. Over the next few chapters, we will find out how much their society changed over a very short space of time.

Letters to Kings and Rulers

As part of his mission and Jihad of Education, the Prophet Muhammad ﷺ sent letters of invitation to Islam to all the surrounding rulers, kings and emperors at the time.

The Negus of Abyssinia (Ethiopia)

"From Muhammad, the Messenger of Allah, to Negus, King of Abyssinia. Peace be upon him who follows true guidance. Salutations, I entertain Allah's praise, there is no God but He, the Sovereign, the Holy, the Source of Peace, the Giver of Peace, the Guardian of Faith, the Preserver of Safety. I bear witness that Jesus, the son of Mary, is the spirit of Allah and His Word which He cast into Mary, the virgin, the good, the pure, so that she conceived Jesus. Allah created him from His Spirit and His breathing as He created Adam by His Hand. I call you to Allah Alone with no associate and to His obedience and to follow me and to believe in that which came to me, for I am the Messenger of Allah. I invite you and your men to Allah, the Glorious, and the All-Mighty. I hereby bear witness that I have communicated my message and advice. I invite you to listen and accept my advice. Peace be upon him who follows true guidance."

Wall murals of saints painted in naive African Christian style in Maryam Papasetti Church, Ethiopia.

The Negus of Abyssinia already had good relations with the Muslims as he had welcomed a group to live there under his protection during the time of the persecution in Makkah.

Some say he accepted Islam when he recived the letter but was met with much resistance by those in the Church.

The Persian Emperor, Khosrow II

The Persian or Sassanid Empire was the second largest empire which stretched across Asia in the time of the Prophet ﷺ.

"In the name of Allah, the Beneficent, the Merciful. From Muhammad, the Messenger of Allah, to Khosrow, the great (leader/head) of the Persians. Peace be upon him, who seeks truth and expresses belief in Allah and in His Prophet and testifies that there is no god but Allah and that He has no partner, and who believes that Muhammad is His servant and Prophet. Under the Command of Allah, I invite you to Him. He has sent me for the guidance of all people so that I may warn them all of His Wrath and may present the unbelievers with an ultimatum. Embrace Islam so that you may remain safe (in this life and the next). And if you refuse to accept Islam, you will be responsible for the sins of the Magi."

Khosrow II was angered that Muhammad's ﷺ name appeared before his and ripped up the letter, sending envoys to bring Muhammad ﷺ before him with no success. The Empire lasted no more than twenty years after this date.

A stone frieze from the Sassanid Empire

The Byzantine Emperor, Flavius Heraclius

15th century painting of Heraclius returning the True Cross to Jerusalem.

"In the name of God, the Most Merciful, the Bestower of all Mercy From Muhammad, Worshipper and Messenger of Allah to Heraclius the Emperor of the Romans:

Peace be upon he who follows the guidance. Furthermore, I invite you with the invitation of peace. If you submit then you will find safety and God will double your reward. If you turn away, you will bear the Arians' sins."

"O People of the Scripture! Come to a common word between us and you: that we shall worship none but God, and that we shall ascribe no partner unto Him, and that none of us shall take others for lords beside God. And if they turn away, then say: Bear witness that we are they who have surrendered (unto Him)." (Aali Imran 3:64).

Heraclius was favourable, according to some accounts, to accept the Prophecy of Muhammad ﷺ, but was met with so much resistance at court, that he did not follow through with his intention.

Other world leaders:

The Governor of Bahrain and the ruler of Oman accepted Islam. The original letter is displayed in the National Museum of Oman and is a source of great happiness to the Muslims there.

The Muqawqis of Egypt

The original letter to the Muqawqis of Egypt which was preserved in a Christian monastery in Egypt. It was sold to an orientalist who sold it to the Ottoman Sultan Abdul Majid who stored it in the Topkapi Palace.

The Muqawqis placed it in an ivory box, to be kept safely in the government treasury and replied, *"From Muqawqis, I read your letter and understood what you have written. I know that the coming of a prophet is still due. But I thought he would be born in Syria - I have treated your messenger with respect and honour. I am sending two maids for you as presents. These maids belong to a very respectable family amongst us. In addition I send clothes for you and a Duldul (steed) for riding. May God bestow security on you."*

"In the name of Allah the Compassionate, the Merciful. From the Apostle of Allah to the Muqawqis, chief of the Copts. Peace be upon him who follows the guidance. Next, I summon thee with the appeal of establishing peace (or submitting your will to Allah): establish peace (submit your will to Allah) and you will have peace. Allah shall give you your reward twofold. But if you decline then on you is the guilt of the Copts. O ye people of the Book, come unto an equal arrangement between us and you, that we should serve none save Allah, associating nothing with Him, and not taking one another for lords besides Allah. And if ye decline, then bear witness that we have submitted our will to Allah."

Social Change - *Jihad of the Hand*

"Spend in charity for your own good. He who remains safe from his own greed will prosper." (At-Tabaghun 64:16)

The Prophet Muhammad ﷺ was able to build the foundations of a new, just and safe society within his lifetime, based on the revelations in the Qur'an.

THE PROPHET ﷺ LED BY EXAMPLE

The Prophet Muhammad ﷺ himself was the example which everyone followed. His mercy, kindness and compassion to all were noticeable. He loved the poor and needy so much that each day he gave all his money to the poor, often leaving nothing for himself for food the next day. As soon as he was informed of an injustice, need or problem, he would do his best to resolve it. The Companion, Anas ﺭ relates that:

"Any of the female slaves in Medina could take the hand of the Messenger of Allah ﷺ and lead him wherever she wished until what she needed was taken care of."

The Prophet ﷺ and his Companions would work tirelessly to build the infrastructure required so that everyone felt safe, protected and cared for.

Prophet Muhammad ﷺ said, "Those I love most among you and those who will sit nearest to me on the Day of Rising are the best of you in character - those who give shelter, those who protect and bring together."
(At-Tirmidhi)

THE CONSTITUTION OF MEDINA

Soon after the Prophet ﷺ arrived in Medina, he gathered all the tribes that lived there, including the Jewish tribes, and created the Constitution (or legal agreement) of Medina. This was the first constitution to be written in recorded history.

The Constitution ended bitter rivalries between some of the tribes because the Prophet ﷺ himself became the mediator. Everyone got a fair hearing and age-old disputes were resolved.

The Constitution established peaceful laws and mutual respect. There were also guidelines for fair trading.

There were laws forbidding any of the tribes to ally with tribes outside Medina.

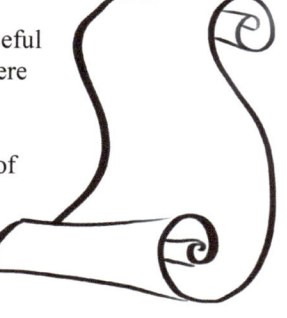

(A full translation can be found in appendix III at the back of the book.)

A NEW AND FAIR JUSTICE SYSTEM

"God commands justice and fair dealing…" (An-Nahl 16:90)

In Arab society before Islam, if someone outside your tribe killed a member of your family then the killer's tribal chief would protect them and nothing would happen. The murder would then spark a blood fued potentially lasting generations. This did not give justice to the victims and produced long term animosity between large groups of people. So instead, under the new rules, if someone killed someone else, they were held personally accountable, not hiding behind their tribal chief. Now the killer would be given a fair trial and a hearing by an authorised judge, notably someone like 'Ali ibn al-Talib ﻮ who would listen to all sides of the case. It was narrated from 'Usamah bin Sharik that the Messenger of Allah ﷺ said, "No person will be punished because of another's crimes."

The U.S. Supreme Court of Justice included the Prophet Muhammad ﷺ in a stone frieze honouring great law givers. The sculptor, knowing it is prohibited in Islam to depict the Prophet Muhammad ﷺ, made a version that was respectful but not intended to look like him.

17th Century Moghul miniature of a court of law.

"Indeed, Allah commands you to render trusts to whom they are due and when you judge between people to judge with justice. Excellent is that which Allah instructs you. Indeed, Allah is ever Hearing and Seeing."
(An-Nisa 4:58)

"O you who have believed, be persistently standing firm in justice, witnesses for Allah, even if it be against yourselves or parents and relatives. Whether one is rich or poor, Allah is more worthy of both."

(An- Nisa 4:135)

Women's Rights

In Arabia, before Islam, women had no rights. They were considered inferior and were more like possessions. A man could marry as many women as he liked, and have as many extra women as well. When a man died, his sons inherited his wives, (except his own mother). Baby girls were sometimes buried in the sand. Allah ﷻ sent revelations to the Prophet Muhammad ﷺ to correct these injustices. For instance, Allah ﷻ reveals His Anger about the practice of burying female babies in this verse of the Qur'an:

"When the sun shall be darkened, when the stars shall be thrown down, when the mountains shall be set moving, when the pregnant camels shall be neglected, when the savage beasts shall be mustered, when the seas shall be set boiling, when the souls shall be coupled, when the buried infant shall be asked for what sin she was slain, when the scrolls shall be unrolled."
(At-Taqwir 81:1)

HOW DID THE PROPHET ﷺ TREAT WOMEN?

The Prophet ﷺ was always very kind and loving towards his wives, always treating them well, never shouting or complaining. He said to his male Companions, *"The best of you are the best to their women."* (Narrated by 'Abdullah ibn Amr.)

His first wife Khadija ر was his constant companion and support during the early years of his prophethood and was incredibly kind, generous and of an extremely high spiritual level. The Prophet ﷺ said about her, *"Mary, the daughter of Imran, was the best among the women (of the world of her time) and Khadijah is the best amongst the women (of this nation)."* (al-Bukhari)

When the Prophet's ﷺ daughter, Fatima ر, entered the room, he ﷺ would stand and sit her beside him and say, *"Fatima is part of me, whoever pleases her, pleases me".*

(al-Bukhari)

The Prophet ﷺ was respectful to all women. In another narration, there was a certain point where the women felt that the men had taken all of the Prophet's ﷺ time, and they too wanted to hear his blessed teachings without vying with a crowd of men, and said openly, *"Messenger of Allah, the men have taken complete possession of your company, so devote one of your days to us."* The Prophet ﷺ promised to give them a day and he preached and

THE NEW LAWS

- Killing newborn baby girls is prohibited
- Unlimited polygamy is banned
- Daughters have rights to inheritance
- Sons do not inherit their father's wives
- Women have the right to divorce
- Marriage has to be consensual
- Men can marry up to four women if they can treat them equally and have the money to do so. (This was primarily for protection in those days.)

gave them instruction. (Bukhari on the authority of Abu Said.)

For the first time in Arabia, women were seen as equal to men, but having different reponsibilities and duties. Men for instance have more responsibility to provide for their families with women being best suited to care for the children and community.

Women also became judges, scholars, business women, teachers and even warriors. A woman was allowed to keep her own money and name after being married and granted the right to divorce. Women were suddenly raised in rank, thanks to the guidance received from the Qur'an and the example of the Prophet ﷺ.

MENTIONING WOMEN IN THE QUR'AN

Umm Salama ﻬ once asked the Prophet ﷺ why, exactly, it seemed sometimes as though God only spoke to men in the Qur'an? The response came soon after:

"For the men who acquiesce to the will of God, and the women who acquiesce,
the men who believe and the women who believe,
the men who are devout and the women who are devout,
the men who are truthful and the women who are truthful,
the men who are constant and the women who are constant,
the men who are humble and the women who are humble,
the men who give charity and the women who give charity,
the men who fast and the women who fast,
the men who are chaste and the women who are chaste,
and the men and women who remember God often, God has arranged forgiveness for them, and a magnificent reward." (Al-Ahzab 33:35)

Painting of a Girl Reading Qur'an by Osman Hamdi Bey

SOCIAL SECURITY

There was no social security before Islam in Arabia. There was much poverty and hunger. An unmarried/ divorced woman would have very few choices about how to survive. Men with no work would have to beg and when they grew old they had to rely on younger members of the family to support them if they were able to.

THE NEW LAWS

- Establishing a communal pot, where charity and tax (2.5% of savings, jizya, import and export tax) is collected and distributed to the poor and needy and for the running of society.
- Helping and protecting the poor and the orphans is highly encouraged.
- Pensions for older men who could not work.
- Families with children received extra food if they needed it.
- Homeless shelters provided for those without homes and money.

Prophet Muhammad ﷺ said, "The one who cares for an orphan and myself will be like this,' and he held his two fingers together to illustrate." *(al-Bukhari)*

Prophet Muhammad ﷺ said, "The one who looks after a widow or a poor person is like: 1) A Mujahid (warrior) who fights for Allah's cause. 2) Like one who performs the prayers all night and 3) Fasts the entire day." *(al-Bukhari)*

Once Sa'd (bin Abi Waqqas) thought that he was superior to those who were below him in rank. On that, the Prophet Muhammad ﷺ said, "You gain no victory or livelihood except through (the blessings and prayers) of the poor amongst you." *(al-Bukhari)*

Slavery

Before Islam, slaves had no rights. They were treated roughly and as possessions. They may not have been given proper clothes, food or shelter, just enough to allow them to work.

"All humans are descended from Adam and Eve. There is no superiority of an Arab over a non-Arab, or of a non-Arab over an Arab, and no superiority of a white person over a black person or of a black person over a white person, except on the basis of personal piety and righteousness." The Prophet Muhammad's ﷺ Farewell Speech

THE NEW LAWS

- Slaves have new legal rights to be protected and treated well.
- They must be given the same standard of food, clothing and shelter as found in their district and ideally the same as their master.
- Recognised as fellow human beings
- Have religious duties
- It is not permitted to make new slaves, i.e. to capture a free man and make them a slave.
- Recommended to free slaves for many heavenly rewards.
- If a slave woman gave birth to her master's child, she and her child were to be granted their freedom.

HOW WERE SLAVES TREATED BY THE PROPHET MUHAMMAD ﷺ?

There was no difference, in the Prophet's ﷺ estimation, between a slave and a free man. He spoke to both with interest and compassion. The slaves were some of his first followers and close Companions. The Prophet ﷺ was most disturbed if one of them was treated badly because of their new faith. The Prophet ﷺ and his Companions would purchase the slaves who were Muslim from their owners, and give them their freedom. He viewed himself as one of them, even though he was from a high born family.

The Prophet Muhammad ﷺ said: *"I am a slave. I eat as a slave eats and I sit as a slave sits."*

The new laws did not ban slavery outright; it was an embedded system, but by prohibiting forcing anyone into slavery, slavery should have died out very soon after the advent of Islam. However, history shows us that there was still slave-trading amongst the Islamic lands until the time of the Ottoman's when it was finally outlawed completely.

Some notable former slave Companions of the Prophet ﷺ include: Bilal ibn Rabah ر, Zayd ibn Harith ر (who became the Prophet's adopted son), Maria al-Qibtiyya ر, and Saffiyyah bint Huyayy ر whom he freed and married, becoming one of the Mothers of the Believers, as the Prophet's ﷺ wives were known.

RULES OF TRADING

"Believers, have fear of God and give up whatever unlawful interest you still demand from others, if you are indeed true believers." (Al-Baqara 2:278)

THE BALANCE BETWEEN SOCIALISM AND CAPITALISM

According to the new rules, free trade was encouraged. A business person (male or female) could make as much money as they liked as long as they made the money lawfully and gave away portions to charity.

A basic tax, or *zakat*, was charged at 2.5% on savings. This *zakat* was collected and distributed to the poor and needy as well as to necessary social infrastructure like new public buildings.

Sadaqa, or voluntary charity, was strongly encouraged, with many wealthy merchants giving large portions of their wealth to help those in need, notably Abu Bakr ﺭ, who gave all of his wealth for the sake of Islam.

The Prophet Muhammad ﷺ said, *"Whoever would like Allah to shade him with His Shade, let him give respite to the one in difficulty, or waive repayment of the loan."*

THE NEW LAWS

- Interest rates on loans are no longer chargeable. (It was normal in those days to charge a 100% interest rate).
- False contracts and dishonest trading is made illegal.
- Trades had inspections and licenses to ensure high standards.
- Caravans could not sell outside the town to avoid being made to sell at a low price.
- A 'free market' was established where the marketplace did not have constructed buildings, only tents so that traders were not charged tax or rent which allowed free trade to develop.

"Is it they who would portion out the Mercy of your Lord? It is We Who portion out between them their livelihood in this world, and We raised some of them above others in ranks, so that some may employ others in their work. But the Mercy (Paradise) of your Lord (O Muhammad ﷺ) is better than the (wealth of this world) which they amass." (Az-Zukhruf 43:32)

In this verse, Allah ﷻ says that He has made different people in different roles so that some can employ others. It also warns of excessive love and hoarding of wealth because this leads to oppression.

The Structure of Society

Finally, the structure of society had changed so that a person was not just a part of their tribe but belonged to a whole community.

The Prophet ﷺ liked both men and women to be doing jobs that they were good at and would recommend jobs and posts, giving all the clans equal access even though some traditionally had a monopoly on some trades like jewellery making. The Prophet ﷺ encouraged training and learning a profession. What would be your ideal job?

TRADERS AND MERCHANTS

If you like traveling and business then this could be for you. Merchants would trade from many foreign lands, by sea and by land.

They would trade silks, perfumes, pottery, dates, jewellery, weapons, medicines and herbs.

GOVERNMENT AND ADMINISTRATIVE JOBS

Vizir Adviser. You have to be very wise and trustworthy for this.

Governor Sent to various provinces to manage that area.

Bookkeeper Accounting was done of the Prophet's ﷺ accounts and the Bayt al-Mal to ensure transparency. Hadrat Bilal ؓ had this role. This job needs high attention to detail and to be good at maths.

Registrar of births, deaths and soldiers. Every person was registered when born and all children from the age of two were entitled to a form of child benefit, usually food. They also kept lists of army volunteers so that the families were looked after if they died. Also so that no-one would join the army if they were underage.

Foreign ambassadors If you are attractive in both look and speech and love communicating, this could be the job for you.

Writers of official documents Those who were very good at writing official documents and treaties, being sensitive to different customs in the various tribes and foreign nations.

Chief of protocol To teach others how to speak or behave when in an audience with the Prophet ﷺ. Sayyidina Abu Bakr ؓ had this role.

Trading standards administrator Ensured fair trading was taking place.

Regent The person put in charge of Medina when the Prophet ﷺ had to leave for battle or otherwise.

Tax collectors Ensuring everyone with savings pays the 2.5% for the poor and needy for the Muslims, the fixed *jizya* tax for non-Muslims and import/export taxes as well as land tax.

Military envoys Sent to explore the region, scouting out for possible attacks. Includes secret missions. Also to learn about innovative war strategies and weapons from other countries.

Dissuaders To go to the enemy to convince them to not fight.

Bodyguards To protect the Prophet ﷺ.

Police Keeping the streets safe.

Manager of endowments Gifts for specific purposes like building schools.

Important note: Positions of power only lasted for four years.

FARMERS

Date farmer was most common
Shepherds
Date pickers
Livestock keeper
Slaughterer

RELIGIOUS AND JUSTICE

Imam leading the prayers and advising the congregation
Qur'an teacher (paid by the government).
Teachers of Fiqh or the Divine Law
Spokesperson for legal matters, like an attorney or court administrator
Judge

CRAFTS

Jewellery maker
Fabric weaver
Tailor
Perfume maker
Potter
Candlemaker
Flag and banner maker
Leatherworker or tanner
Builder or carpenter
Blacksmith

SERVICES AND HOSPITALITY

Owner of inns and houses for travelers
Cook or catering
Manager of the poor lodge or homeless shelter.
Scribe - those with good handwriting
Water seller
Water diviner - finding places for wells.
Swimmer - to help people across water.
Woodman
Beautician
Marriage matchmaker
Barber
Horse, camel and pet keeper
Money exchanger
Property surveyor
Desert guide

HEALTHCARE

You could work in Medina at the Prophet's Mosque where sick people were treated.

Doctor Medicine had made huge advances. The Prophet ﷺ would recommend various herbs, treatments and passages of the Holy Qur'an. Quarantine was also used in the case of infectious diseases and distancing measures were put in place.
Nurse Nurses could be hired and were present on the battlefields.
Midwife

PENAL SYSTEM

Police were employed to catch people who were a threat to society and to keep the streets safe. If someone had to go to prison because they were a danger to others, the prisons had to follow humanitarian guidelines. According to Shar'iah, prison guards could not use torture, nor could the prisoner be confined to small dark spaces with no windows or to be put into isolation. Clothing and meals had to be provided. There were prisons for both men and women. For those repeatedly committing crimes then often banishment from the city was ordered. For very serious crimes: execution.

The Struggle of the Self - *Jihad of the Heart*

THE PURPOSE OF RELIGIOUS TEACHINGS

"We are now returning from the lesser Jihad to the greater Jihad, the Jihad against the self."

(Hadith in Al-Ghazali - Ihya')

Nafaḥāt al-Uns ('Breaths of Intimacy'17th century) Many verses in the Qur'an and stories from Islamic teachers are in the form of allegory or hidden meanings. This painting shows dogs waiting obediently outside, hinting at the taming of our lower desires. The peacock may represent the danger of pride and the tree and gardens behind the door show a possibility of inner Paradise.

The main purpose of religion is to guide people to God. In Islam, this is done through the Purification of the Self, or *Tazkiyyat al-Nafs*. The Prophet Muhammad ﷺ spent his life guiding and teaching those around him. The inner Jihad, the Jihad of the Heart or the Jihad al-Nafs, is central to Islam.

The early Muslims would engage in inner Jihad by praying, fasting and following the ways taught by the Prophet ﷺ.

In the Prophet's ﷺ Farewell Pilgrimage speech, he said: *"The Fighter in the Way of Allah is he who makes Jihad against himself (Jihada Nafsah) for the sake of obeying Allah." (Tirmidhi, Ahmad, al-Hakim)*

Many people have characteristics that prevent them from being peaceful in themselves and being close to Allah. The perfection of character, of purifying the self through self-discipline and good actions, paves the way towards knowing Allah in this life.

SECLUSION IN THE CAVE

Before his prophethood was revealed, Muhammad ﷺ used to spend long amounts of time in seclusion in the Cave of Hira. There he meditated and thought about his Lord. This is where, when the Prophet ﷺ was 40 years old, the Angel Jibrael عليهوسلم came to him and revealed the first surah of the Qur'an.

The Cave of Hira, where the Holy Prophet Muhammad ﷺ received his first revelation of Qur'an.

A VISIT FROM THE ANGEL JIBRAEL TO TEACH ISLAM, IMAN AND IHSAN

Angel Jibrael عليهوسلم visited the Prophet ﷺ every time part of the Qur'an was revealed. One time he came in human form as we hear below in the famous hadith narrated by Sayyidina 'Umar ﺭ:

"We were sitting with the Prophet ﷺ when a man came to him whose clothes were intensely white and whose hair was intensely black; no signs of travel could be seen upon him, and none of us recognized him. He sat down facing the Prophet ﷺ, with his knees touching his, and he put his hands on his thighs, and said: 'O Muhammad, what is *Islam*?'

He ﷺ said: 'To testify that none has the right to be worshipped but Allah, and that I am the Messenger of Allah, to establish regular prayer, to pay Zakat, to fast in Ramadan, and to perform Hajj to the House (the Ka'bah).'

The man said: 'You have spoken the truth.' We were amazed by him: He asked a question, then told him that he had spoken the truth.

Then he asked: 'O Muhammad, what is *Iman,* faith?

He ﷺ said: 'To believe in Allah, His Angels, His Messengers, His Books, the Last Day, and the Divine Decree (Qadar), both the good of it and the bad of it.'

The man said,' You have spoken the truth.'

Then he said: 'O Muhammad, what is *Ihsan*?' (Right action, goodness, sincerity)

The Prophet ﷺ said: 'To worship Allah as if you see Him, for even though you do not see Him, He sees you.'

The Prophet ﷺ met me three days later and asked me: 'Do you know who that man was?'

An artists' impression of the Archangel Michael from Mamluk period. Displayed at the Metropolitan Museum of Art.

I said, 'Allah and His Messenger know best.' He said: 'That was Jibrael عليهوسلم, who came to you to teach you your religion.'"

This hadith shows that there are different spiritual levels that people can achieve. The three levels of Islam, Iman and Ihsan form the path of enlightenment.

The first, *Islam*, is to know well the foundations of the religion, what is right and what is wrong, according to the Divine Law. The second, *Iman*, is to perfect the belief in Allah ﷻ. Finally, the seeker reaches a level of *Ihsan*, where he or she arrives at the point of true awareness or consciousness of Allah ﷻ which relates to the verse:

"And I did not create the Jinn and Mankind except to worship Me." (Ad-Dhariyat 51:56)

How Did the Prophet ﷺ Teach His Companions?

The Prophet ﷺ would teach and guide his Companions so that they could develop good character and draw closer to Allah ﷻ. The Prophet ﷺ taught that practising patience in different situations was the key to success. He would often teach by way of stories.

Imagine someone comes up and begins to insult your best friend, what would you do? In this hadith, a man comes to insult the Prophet ﷺ, and the Prophet's ﷺ best friend Abu Bakr ﵁ is sitting with him. The man started to say all sorts of terrible things to the Prophet ﷺ, both the Prophet ﷺ and Abu Bakr ﵁ remained silent. Then, Abu Bakr ﵁ could not contain himself any longer and directed some insults in return. The Prophet ﷺ then got up and left. Abu Bakr ﵁ followed the Prophet ﷺ and asked, "Why did you leave?" The Prophet ﷺ replied:

"An angel was with you, responding on your behalf. But when you said back to him some of what he said, a devil arrived, and it is not for me to sit with devils."

This shows the difficulty in being patient and holding the tongue, even for someone like Abu Bakr as-Siddique ﵁. Abu Bakr ﵁ would sometimes put a stone in his mouth to remind him to not speak unnecessarily, such was his sincerity.

Behzad's Advice of the Ascetic (c. 1500-1550)

TESTS IN LIFE

Sometimes very difficult things happen in life. The early Muslims were taught about how this life is a trial or test and to have patience with Allah's Decree:

On the authority of Abu Hurayrah (may Allah be pleased with him), who said that the Messenger of Allah ﷺ said: "Allah (mighty and sublime be He) says: 'My faithful servant's reward from Me, if I have taken to Me his best friend from amongst the inhabitants of the world and he has then borne it patiently for My sake, shall be nothing less than Paradise.'" (al-Bukhari)

The Prophet ﷺ himself experienced great loss, of his family and his home and community, but was patient and thankful, even in his most difficult times. The Prophet ﷺ had such excellence of character, that even during extreme adversity he did not complain, become angry or feel sorry for himself. He was a living example for his Companions and for all Muslims, of how to be trustworthy, kind, loyal, pious, generous, forbearing, patient and thankful; he was a model of perfection.

"Allah loves those who purify themselves." (At-Tawbah 9:108)

THE BEST OF ACTIONS

The Prophet ﷺ said: "Shall I tell you something that is the best of all deeds, constitutes the best act of piety in the eyes of your Lord, elevates your rank in the hereafter, and carries more virtue than the spending of gold and silver in the service of Allah, or taking part in Jihad and slaying or being slain in the path of Allah?"
They said: "Yes!"
He said: "Remembrance of Allah." (Ahmad, Tirmidhi)

Remembrance of Allah helps a Muslim turn away from selfish and negative actions and helps to purify the soul. If a Muslim is granted success by Allah ﷻ in their struggle against the ego, they can arrive at a state where Allah says through a hadith of the Prophet ﷺ:

On the authority of Abu Hurayrah (may Allah be pleased with him), who said that the Messenger of Allah ﷺ said: "Allah (mighty and sublime be He) said: 'Whosoever shows enmity to someone devoted to Me, I shall be at war with him. My servant draws not near to Me with anything more loved by Me than the religious duties I have enjoined upon him, and My servant continues to draw near to Me with supererogatory works so that I shall love him. When I love him I am his hearing with which he hears, his seeing with which he sees, his hand with which he strikes and his foot with which he walks. Were he to ask [something] of Me, I would surely give it to him, and were he to ask Me for refuge, I would surely grant him it...'" (al-Bukhari - hadith Qudsi no. 25)

The Jihad of the Heart was initially called 'the purification of the self' and later called *Tasawwuf*, and according to traditional Islamic Scholars, is one of the three *fard* (obligatory) types of knowledge in Islam, as we heard earlier in the hadith about the Angel Jibrael; that of the Divine Law, *Islam*, perfecting belief, *Iman* and the purification of the self, *Ihsan*, which removes the negative characteristics of anger, pride and lust. Traditionally in Islam, following the model set by the Prophet ﷺ, all sacred sciences are learnt under a qualified teacher or sheikh.

"They arise from [their] beds; they supplicate their Lord in fear and aspiration, and from what We have provided them, they spend. And no soul knows what has been hidden for them of comfort for their eyes as reward for what they used to do."

(As-Sajda 32:16-17)

Military & Defence - *Jihad of the Sword*

The Jihad of the Sword is what most people think of when they hear the word Jihad. The Prophet ﷺ only engaged in Jihad of the Sword when the command (from Allah ﷻ) came to protect the Muslims who were in danger of being annihilated after years of persecution.

CONDITIONS IN MAKKAH

In the hostile environment of Makkah, the Quraysh tried every means to intimidate the Prophet ﷺ and the early Muslims.

The Prophet Muhammad ﷺ, so far, had been engaged with Jihad of Education and Counsel, mostly in secret with the few early followers. The new Muslims were mercilessly persecuted by the Makkans, some of them being tortured or even killed. Most Makkans saw Islam as a threat to their way of life, with idol worship having been established for hundreds of years. People resist change and none more so than the Quraysh of Makkah. Some Makkans hated the Muslims with a passion, notably Abu Jahl and Abu Lahab. Abu Lahab even tried to kill the Prophet ﷺ with a stone. If it was not for the protection of Abu Talib, the Prophet's ﷺ uncle, he would not have been able to remain in Makkah for as long as he did, such was the threat on his life. Bear in mind though it was not Prophet Muhammad ﷺ himself they hated, but what he preached, because it meant they would have to leave their old ways behind.

The Makkans decided to impose a four-year boycott on the Banu Hashim, the Prophet's ﷺ clan, where they were banished from the main town and could not trade or marry. They became very poor and often had little food.

Throughout these difficulties, the Prophet ﷺ never sought to take revenge, but patiently endured and continued to peacefully preach about the Oneness of Allah. They were eventually allowed to return to Makkah but the persecution continued.

Finally, the opposing clans of the Quraysh got together and made a plan to kill the Prophet ﷺ. If they managed to kill him as a group of all the clans, they could avoid a long-term blood feud with the Bani Hashim, because one clan could not be blamed. In their meeting, they decided that one member from each clan would secretly go during the night and kill the Prophet ﷺ while he slept.

Allah informed the Prophet ﷺ by a revelation and in the evening he made preparations to migrate to Medina, about two hundred miles

A statue or Nabataean Baetyl of an idol, possibly al-Uzza, who was mentioned in the Qur'an. There were hundreds of idols installed inside the Ka'aba for the pagan pilgrims to come and worship.

north of Makkah with his closest Companion, Abu Bakr ﺭ. The people of Medina, which was then called Yathrib, invited the Prophet ﷺ to stay at the second Bai'at al-Aqaba where they gave him their allegiance. Many of them had embraced Islam and were keen for him to make his base in their city.

MIGRATION TO MEDINA

That evening, 'Ali ﺭ agreed to sleep in the bed of the Prophet ﷺ. As night fell, the Prophet ﷺ and Abu Bakr ﺭ were able to leave undetected, and made their way across the desert, towards Medina, covering their tracks as they went, intending to rest in a small cave on the way.

Meanwhile, the Makkans stormed into the Prophet's ﷺ room only to find 'Ali ibn Abu Talib ﺭ laying there instead. They furiously searched the town and realising the Prophet ﷺ must have left, they organised a search party the next morning, using the best desert tracker in Makkah.

"If you do not aid the Prophet - Allah has already aided him when those who disbelieved had driven him out (of Makkah) as one of two, when they were in the cave and he said to his companion, 'Do not grieve; indeed Allah is with us ' And Allah sent down His tranquillity upon him and supported him with angels you did not see and made the word of those who disbelieved the lowest, while the Word of Allah - that is the highest. And Allah is Exalted in Might and Wise." (At-Tawbah 9:40)

THE CAVE

Abu Bakr ﺭ and Muhammad ﷺ had found the cave they planned to rest in. They waited to see if the Makkans would pass by. Even though they had covered their tracks, the Makkans came perilously close to the cave. Before they arrived, accounts tell of a dove who built her nest and a spider who built a large web across the entrance to the cave. The Makkans, seeing this, thought there was no way anyone could be inside the cave and moved off.

That night, Abu Bakr's ﺭ daughter 'Asma ﺭ, who knew the location of the cave, was able to smuggle food and two camels out of Makkah for her father and the Prophet ﷺ.

The Prophet ﷺ and Abu Bakr ﺭ resumed their journey and finally, tired and exhausted, arrived in Medina amid great welcome and cheers. The Medinites, already many believing in the Prophet's ﷺ mission, welcomed him with open arms, and Muhammad ﷺ made this his home from then on. Muslims from Makkah also began to make the migration to Medina, making Medina the new Muslim centre.

LEAD UP TO THE BATTLE OF BADR

The Makkans however were not content that Muhammad ﷺ had left the city. They knew he would be gaining numbers and influence in Medina. Over the next two years, they sent small groups to attack outlying areas around Medina, as well as sending a formal threat to the Medinites that they should either turn the Prophet ﷺ out of their lands or be ready to face the armies of the Makkans who would destroy them.

The Medinites of course would not do this so the Quraysh discussed among themselves how best to remove the threat of Islam. They eventually decided to invest in a good army and prepared a trade caravan to go to Syria so that they could use all the profits to make weapons and armour. Even the

> *"The Prophet ﷺ invited the unbelievers to Islam peacefully, lodged protests against their beliefs, and strove to remove their misgivings about Islam. When they refused any other solution, but rather declared war against him and his message and initiated the fight, there was no alternative but to fight back."*
>
> Sa'id Ramadan Buti, an orthodox scholar of Islam

A Persian painting of the incident of the cave, 17th Century.

women, who were not normally interested in trading, donated their possessions and so it was a very richly laden caravan.

On it's return, the caravan would pass within a few miles of Medina. Abu Sufyan ﺭ* became anxious about this and sent a messenger to alert Makkah about this potential threat. The message was much exaggerated which caused alarm amongst the Quraysh as they thought a great number of Muslims were about to attack it and so immediately prepared one thousand men to fight them. They decided to attack on the 18th of Ramadan. The Prophet ﷺ was informed that the Makkan army was mobilised and he consulted both the Ansar and the Muhajireen who unanimously agreed, there was no other choice but to meet the Quraysh in battle.

Story of the Battle of Badr

As told by a fictional character, 'Abdul Karim, 19 years old, who relates his experiences of the events recorded at the Battle of Badr which took place on the 18th Ramadan 2 A.H. (623 C.E.).

Word was spreading around Medina that morning that the head of the Quraysh clan, Abu Sufyan, had a huge caravan loaded with riches and he would be passing nearby. I ran to find my friends. "Let's raid the caravan, we'll be rich!" I said.

"No way, Abdul Karim!" said my closest friend, Harith. "Don't you know it's Abu Sufyan's? He'll come and cut off your head!"

We all laughed.

"Let's see if we can spot it—I'll race you to the hill!" 'The hill' was our favourite lookout point on the edge of Medina.

"You won't be able to beat me!" said Shamsuddin who was the fastest runner.

We all sped away at top speed, and although I got a head start, Harith soon caught up with me, laughing as he passed. Shamsuddin also quickly passed me—how could I be so slow? We all arrived panting at the bottom of the hill. Shamsudin had a skin of water that he passed around as we caught our breath.

We climbed to the top of the hill where we could see for miles in the distance, hoping to get a glimpse of the richly laden caravan. I strained my eyes but could just see the rocky hills and desert landscape, flickering under the sun's heat. It must be passing a lot further than we thought.

We stayed there for a little while, standing up occasionally to look again and resting on the rocks until the sun was too hot.

"It's getting close to *dhuhr* prayer, I'm going back," I said. I never used to be interested in praying but when the Prophet ﷺ arrived two years ago, everything had changed; life was exciting.

Last year, I took my *shahada* with the Prophet ﷺ himself. It was an experience I shall never forget. I could hardly look at him, he was so majestic. My heart filled with so much love and I was in awe of his presence. He put me at ease though; he joked with me and ruffled my hair. I would do anything for him.

We made our way home through the market on the edge of Medina. On the town side of the market, there were stalls and rugs laid out on the dusty ground selling sweet-smelling incense, herbs and spices, juicy dates of all types, bread and other foods, clothing and linen, and heavy woven red and orange carpets. The sound of poetry and haggling filled the air.

We came to my favourite stall: the swordsmiths'. We admired one that was beautifully made, engraved with a Persian-looking design with a scabbard made of leather and blue silk. I would not have minded trying it out but had second thoughts as the stall owner appeared. He was a large, aged warrior with a huge beard and a dusty turban resting on his head. He was known for his short temper. Sometimes though, when he was in a good mood, he would tell us about the time he had fought in Makkah when the king and his elephants came to try to destroy the Kaaba. He said Allah had sent birds with small, burning hot stones to destroy the enemy and protect the Holy House.

But today he didn't look in a good mood, so I smiled pleasantly and asked how much some arrow tips were and then left. I took care to avoid the old lady who sat at the edge of the market with her heavily wrinkled face and no teeth. She would try to grab people's clothes and tell them their fortune. It says in the Qur'an that fortune-telling and divination is prohibited. The market used to be full of people hoping to tell you your destiny for half a dirham.

Beggars lined the edges of the market. I felt sorry for them but at least now there would be some

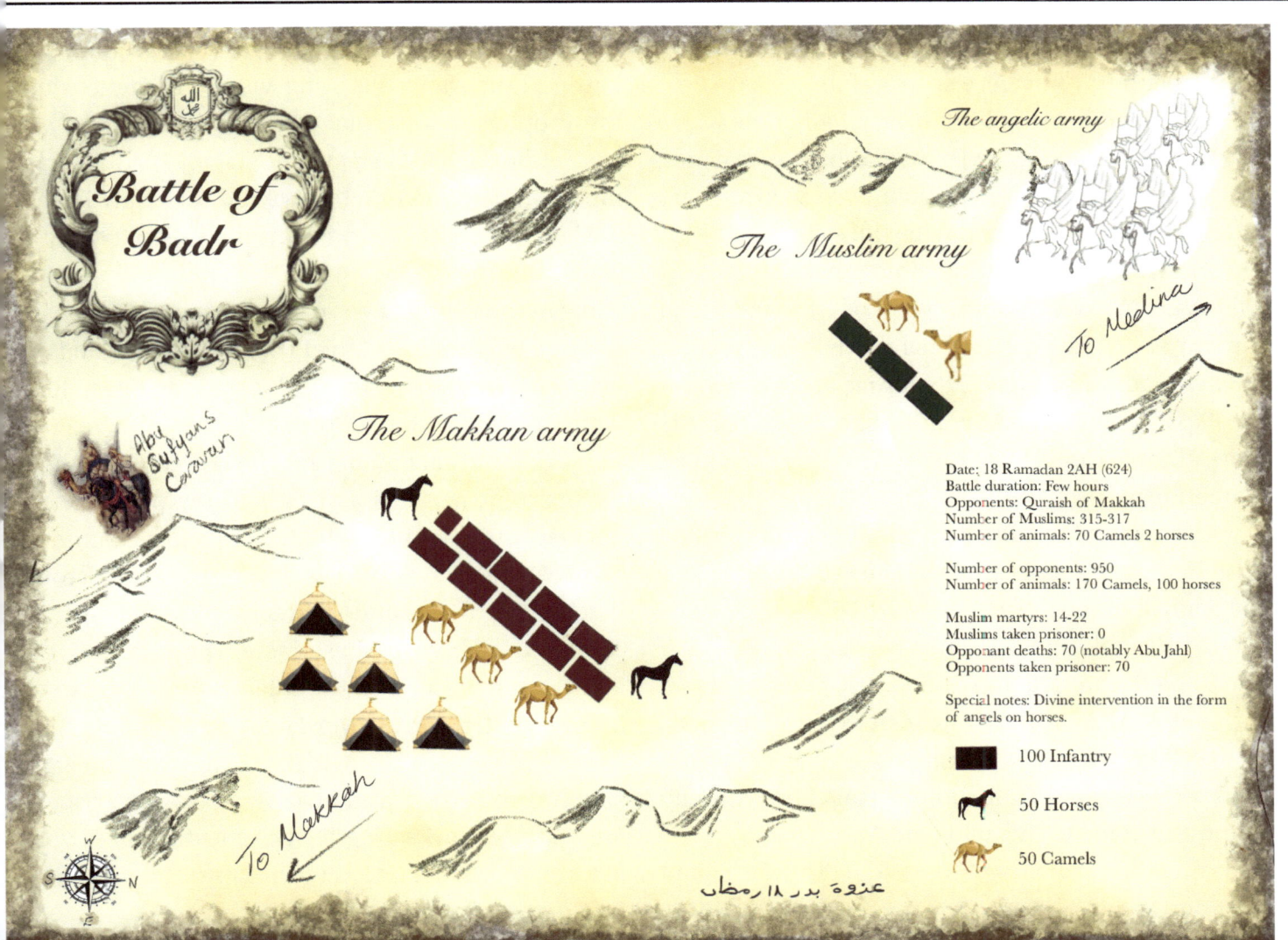

Battle of Badr

The angelic army

The Muslim army

The Makkan army

Abu Sufyan's Caravan

To Medina

To Makkah

Date: 18 Ramadan 2AH (624)
Battle duration: Few hours
Opponents: Quraish of Makkah
Number of Muslims: 315-317
Number of animals: 70 Camels 2 horses

Number of opponents: 950
Number of animals: 170 Camels, 100 horses

Muslim martyrs: 14-22
Muslims taken prisoner: 0
Opponent deaths: 70 (notably Abu Jahl)
Opponents taken prisoner: 70

Special notes: Divine intervention in the form of angels on horses.

100 Infantry

50 Horses

50 Camels

---

food provided for them at the Prophet's ﷺ Mosque and by the Muslims, whenever they could. The Prophet ﷺ told us that there were so many heavenly blessings for feeding the poor.

Pungent smells of camel dung surrounded the outer part of the market. Camels, horses, sheep and goats were being bought and sold. Bedouins would arrive from the desert with their camels, their clothes dirty and unkept, trading and bargaining what they could.

I arrived at my house to wash and get ready to go to the Mosque.

"*As-salaamu 'alaikum,* Abdul Karim," Shukur greeted me as I pushed the fabric hanging aside that covered our front door and stepped into my house. It was a two-storey building that my father and my uncle made before I was born. It was made of mud and wood. Shakur was the father of the family from Makkah whom we agreed could stay with us. When everyone arrived from Makkah to escape the troubles there, the people of Medina offered to share their homes and their provisions. The Prophet ﷺ called us the *Ansar* - the Helpers -because of our generosity.

"'*Alaikum as-salaam,* Shakur," I said and sighed as I saw my bow and arrow had been moved again. His son, Shamil, aged ten, tended to use my belongings a little too much and without my permission. I also had to sleep in my parent's room so Shakur and his family could stay in my room. My mother hung a large piece of material between my bed and theirs to give us all some privacy.

Shakur was an African slave in Makkah. When he and his wife became Muslim, they endured much hardship. Abu Bakr, may Allah be well pleased with him, one of the Prophet's ﷺ closest Companions, had bought them for a high price and then gave them their freedom. They were so grateful.

I loved hearing his stories of when he was a boy in Africa over dinner. His melodious voice would tell us about his tribe and his family as well as scary tales of witch doctors and tribal lore.

I went upstairs to my room to change. Finding a fairly clean cloak to wear, I went outside and found the water to perform my *wu'du* that my mother always made sure was ready for us, and headed for the Mosque with Shakur and Shamil. My parents were already there. The Holy Prophet ﷺ had called a meeting.

Sa'd ibn Mu'adh, the leader of Medina, called out; "Everyone gather around! The Prophet ﷺ seeks the council of the *Ansar*!"

We gathered and sat in a large group.

Sa'd ibn Mu'adh stood up, and said, "O Prophet of Allah, is it us you wish to speak to?"

The Prophet ﷺ said, "Yes, it is you from whom I wish to hear, for I have travelled from my home and come to live with you."

He informed us that the Quraysh had summoned an army and were heading towards Medina to protect their caravan and that it was very likely they would attack the city. The Prophet ﷺ said we should meet them in battle, and that Angel Jibrail عليهوسلم, had promised us victory. But he, as a guest in our town, wanted to hear from the people of Medina, as he did not want us to get involved in something that was his conflict. Abu Bakr ؓ, Hamza ؓ (the Prophet's ﷺ Uncle), `Umar ؓ, and `Ali ؓ were all ready to defend the Prophet ﷺ —with their lives if need be.

I waited for the answer from the leader of our city.

Sa'd declared, "O Prophet of Allah, may our lives and souls and all our possessions be ransomed in your way!" In other words, the Prophet ﷺ had our complete support.

The Prophet ﷺ was happy with these words. He called Sa'd to him and kissed his face and said, "O Sa'd, may Allah reward you well."

It was decided—we were to prepare for battle. My heart was bursting with excitement to join the Prophet ﷺ in actual combat. I thought of the sword that my father gave me for my birthday last month and all the practice we did together. Then a flash of fear passed through my belly—the reality of war. I had never been in real combat before, and some of the Quraysh were formidable fighters.

I looked over at the Prophet ﷺ again, and my heart filled with peace and courage. Everything would be fine with the Prophet ﷺ on our side.

Waiting at home to leave, I still could not help feeling a bit nervous as I packed my provisions. I decided my sword needed sharpening again so I went outside. I drew the blade over the stone, listening to the sound of steel and stone. I then practised many strokes, faster and faster, the midday sun flashing on the steel. All boys, and some of the girls, trained in sword fighting in Medina from an early age. We also trained in wrestling and shooting the bow. I wanted to be the best warrior in Medina one day. Feeling better, I sheathed my sword in its leather scabbard as I heard my father saying it was time to leave.

My mother waited in the doorway of our house with tears in her eyes but with a look of strength that her newly found faith gave her, filling my heart with even more courage.

My father smiled and hugged my mother and then said to us both: "We are serving a higher goal, for the Prophet's mission, indeed for Allah Himself. May He grant us victory!"

"*Ameen!*" we both replied.

We headed out towards Badr, about two days march from Medina, near where the caravan had passed. The Prophet ﷺ received news that the Quraysh armies were about one hour away and that they had slaughtered nine or ten beasts for food. That meant there were about one thousand men. I looked around and made an approximate count of our army. We only had about three hundred men, but included some of the best fighters in all of Arabia, such as `Ali ibn Talib﷡, `Umar Ibn Khattab﷡ and Hamza﷡.

That night, camping out under the stars near my friends, Harith and Shamsuddin, I barely slept for all the excitement and nervous anticipation. The heavens seemed alive as I gazed into the vast blackness of night.

The next day, the Prophet ﷺ wisely positioned us with mountains to our sides and back to protect our army. He also stopped up the wells and built a water cistern so we would have water, but the enemy wouldn't.

We assumed our positions as the attacking army approached. There were flank after flank of the powerful clans of Makkah, their faces intent on destroying us. There were camels among their cavalry. I looked again at our small number and the reality dawned on me that they outnumbered us three to one. In my mind, I frantically tried to go over all the sword moves and throws that my father and uncle had shown me. I looked over at my friends who were looking serious and probably doing the same thing. Shamsuddin shifted uncomfortably from foot to foot.

Abu Jahl, whom I had heard was the worst of the enemy, called out, "If it is true what Muhammad says, then we are out to fight the God of the Heavens. But who that fights against me, is then fighting the God

of the Heavens!"

"What's that idiot trying to say? That he is Allah?" I wondered aloud in surprise.

"As if!" Harith snorted.

Then a man from the tribe of Bani Makhzum said, "I swear to God that I will drink from the Muslims' cistern, or destroy it or die beside it!"

He ran towards our cistern well, but Hadrat Hamza﷡ tried to prevent him, cutting off his leg. I was shocked. Especially when the man dragged himself and his stump of a leg to the water cistern and threw himself in. Hamza immediately followed and killed him, the waters running with blood. Later, the enemy asked for water from the well, but it was said that everyone who drank from the well that day did not live to see the battle.

We were not to fight that day. Both armies retreated to their camps, planning to meet the next morning in battle. There was much silence as the men found places to camp for the night, each man preparing themselves for what looked like an unmatched battle.

During the evening, the Prophet ﷺ informed us of an *ayat* from the Qur'an:

"If victory you are seeking, victory has already come to you; and if you give over, it is better for you. But if you return, We shall return, and your host will avail you nothing though it be numerous; and that God is with the believers." (The Spoils:19)

Alhamdulillah, this greatly reassured us. That night, as we lay out under the stars, I thought again about the Holy verse.

In the morning, after praying for success, The Prophet ﷺ emerged from his small tent made of palm leaves and organized us into our ranks. I wanted to be right at the front, but new to battle, I was placed towards the rear. Of course, I went where the Prophet ﷺ ordered me to go, privately quite relieved.

As was the custom, the best warriors on both sides stepped forward to a duel. The enemy first sent out Utba bin Rabi'a, Shayba bin Rabi'a, and Walid, his son. They were big, fierce and armored, with more weapons than I thought possible. First, three of our Ansar clan rode out to meet them, but Abu Jahl said he wanted to fight his equals and had no quarrel with the people of Medina. So the Prophet ﷺ sent out `Ali ibn Abi Talib؇, Ubayda bin Harith؇, and Hamza ibn Abdul Muttalib؇ to fight them.

In no time at all, Hadrat `Ali؇ slew Walid; Hadrat Hamza؇ slew Shayba; but Utba cut Hadrat Ubayda's؇ leg off, spilling blood on the sand. `Ali؇ and Hamza؇ finished off Utba, and carried Ubayda؇ to the Holy Prophet ﷺ. The Prophet ﷺ knelt down and said some words to him; we saw Ubayda؇ smile as he died.

The battle began. I saw the Prophet ﷺ in the distance on the front line of the battle; he was bravely fighting off the enemy, one after the other, his close Companions around him. The Prophet ﷺ would push further and further into the midst of the battle, he looked as courageous as a lion, with no sign of fear, even though the Quraysh looked deranged and dark with fury. I prayed to Allah for support and mustered my courage and ran into the enemy, engaging one warrior and then another. An extra power I didn't know I had flowed through me. I felt invincible.

Then a youth my age challenged me. We were matched well, and his sword hit hard on my shield.

As I overpowered him, he came back with an ingenious move, wounding my side. I barely felt the injury and forged on until I struck him with a heavy blow. He retreated and limped away. I could not chase him as there were so many more behind him.

My fellow Muslims were being mortally wounded. Mihja؇ received an arrow in his chest and the Prophet's Companion, Harith؇, an older man, also had his throat pierced by an arrow. Indeed, our numbers seemed few compared to the enemy and they seemed to be gaining much ground.

My next opponent was a large man with a face full of scars. He was experienced and strong and I had to use all my strength to fight him off. He hit my sword so hard that it flew out of my grip and landed a few yards away, so I immediately got him into a headlock and forced him to the ground and held him there, at the same time reaching for my sword.

I looked up and saw the Prophet ﷺ praying to Allah and, to my amazement, scores of angels appeared, descending from the heavens, riding on horses with spears and swords in their hands!

The angels seemed to be made of light, yet powerful and frightening, heading towards the enemy.

The Prophet ﷺ glanced at me for a moment, acknowledging me as a witness. As I was distracted

by this awesome sight, my opponent managed to struggle free and stood up. He saw the surprise on my face and turned to see what I was looking at but did not appear to see anything. He then raised his sword, about to strike me, when suddenly he grew afraid and ran away.

I looked back toward the Prophet ﷺ as he threw a handful of dust at the enemy. This seemed to cause a mighty wind to rise, making me unsteady on my feet. The wind whirled around, collecting sand and small pebbles. It rose higher and higher, then hurled its' tiny weapons into the attackers' faces. At the same time, their necks felt the deadly blows of the angels and many fell dead. My companions and I were amazed as our enemies collapsed at our feet. The rest of them dropped their weapons and ran away.

Something extraordinary had just happened and I was now in even more awe of Allah's ﷻ power and how He had sent His help to us.

That evening, the Prophet ﷺ ordered all the dead bodies of the enemy to be thrown into a dry well. He called out to them, "O people of the pit, you were an evil kinsfolk to your Prophet. You called me a liar and expelled me from your city. Have you found what Allah has promised you is true? I have found that what my Lord promises me is true."

Some people asked him why he was calling to dead bodies, and the Prophet ﷺ said, "They hear as well as you do, but they cannot answer."

We set to work digging the graves of the Muslim Martyrs—those who had died for their religion. A messenger arrived who told us that the Prophet's beloved daughter, Ruqayyah, had died of an illness while we were away. This was indeed sad news. She was beloved to the Prophet ﷺ. I had not met her personally, but heard she was beautiful, kind and pious.

We were allowed some of the spoils from the battle. I was given a piece of armor; it was made of leather and metal and would come in very useful. The Prophet ﷺ told us that before this, the prophets were not allowed to have the spoils of war, but Allah had revealed a new verse of Qur'an that gave him permission.

We also had many prisoners. In normal Arab custom, prisoners were either killed or used as slaves. The Holy Prophet ﷺ announced that instead, we would keep them captive and offer ransoms for them. He did not wish to harm them.

Over the next few weeks, we saw many people from Makkah come to claim their relatives and pay their ransom. We watched them arrive; some looked scared to enter Medina—they didn't know that we Muslims were not going to hurt them. I even heard that if they had no money, the Prophet ﷺ let them go anyway! This was new to all of us; we were not used to kindness in our old ways of warfare. The ransoms brought some much-needed money to our town.

At the *Jum'ah* prayer, the Prophet ﷺ told us about the revelations that he'd received in the battle. I especially remember these:

"When you were calling upon your Lord for help, and he answered you, 'I shall reinforce you with a thousand angels riding behind you.'" (The Spoils: 9)

"When thy Lord was revealing to the angels, I am with you; so confirm the believers. I shall cast into the unbelievers' hearts terror; so smite them above the necks, and smite every finger of them!" (The Spoils, 12)

Memories of the Battle of Badr will stay with me for the rest of my life. I will never forget them.

The Islamic Rules of Battle

War is an unpleasant fact of life, which seems to persist throughout all times in history. Islam is unique in that it recognises this unfortunate situation and has a set code of conduct in battle for those times when there is no other choice. Thanks to the efforts of the early Muslims engaging in combative Jihad, there are clear rules of battle, protecting innocent lives, crops and animals.

The Prophet ﷺ only engaged in battle when:

☒ A clan or group did not respond to diplomacy or listen to reason.

☒ A clan or group was intent on destroying Islam.

☒ A clan or group was intent on fighting.

☒ A clan or group committed an act of treachery.

If a battle had to take place, then the following rules applied: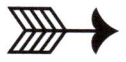

Arab army crossing the desert, ready for battle.

"Do not kill any child, any woman, or any elder or sick person." (Sunan Abu Dawud)

"Do not practice treachery or mutilation." (Al-Muwatta)

"Do not uproot or burn palms or cut down fruitful trees." (Al-Muwatta)

"Do not slaughter a sheep or a cow or a camel, except for food."

(Al-Muwatta)

"If one fights his brother, [he must] avoid striking the face, for God created him in the image of Adam." (Sahih Bukhari, Sahih Muslim)

"Do not kill the monks in monasteries, and do not kill those sitting in places of worship." (Musnad Ahmad Ibn Hanbal)

"Do not destroy the villages and towns, do not spoil the cultivated fields and gardens, and do not slaughter the cattle."

(al-Bukhari, Abu Dawud)

"Do not wish for an encounter with the enemy; pray to God to grant you security; but when you [are forced to] encounter them, exercise patience." (Sahih Muslim)

"No one may punish with fire except the Lord of fire." (Sunan Abu Dawud)

"Do not kill the workers/wage earners (i.e. those workers not fighting you." (Ahmad: 15562)

(Reference to the Prophet's ﷺ saying or hadith in brackets.)

The Story of the Battle of Uhud

'Abdul Karim continues to relate his experiences of the events recorded at the Battle of Uhud on the 7th Shawwal, 2 A.H. (623 C.E.).

Things were stirring in our blessed town of Medina. A whole year had passed since the great Battle of Badr and we had heard that the Quraysh in Makkah were plotting their revenge.

Hubab ibn al-Mundhir and a group of scouts were sent out to find out information about the Makkans. We eagerly waited to hear what news they brought. In the meantime, the women, children and elderly were ordered to withdraw to safe quarters just in case of a sudden attack.

A cry came from the Prophet's ﷺ Mosque: "O leaders of Yathrib, leaders of the Sahaba, your Prophet is calling you to a war meeting. Come at once!"

My father hurried to join the meeting as he was one of the leaders. He returned within an hour and gathered our family around. He looked at me and said, "We must get you ready for battle, my son. The army of Quraysh are encamped by the mountain of Uhud—one day's journey from here. The Prophet ﷺ told us his dream about cattle and his sword."

My mother, who was always interested in dreams, asked, "Can you remember exactly what the dream was?"

My father thought for a moment. "Yes, the Prophet said: 'I saw in my dream a herd of cattle being slaughtered, and I saw a gash open upon the

blade of my sword. Upon my back, I wore a suit of mail, and my hand I stuck into a collar of a suit of mail. The meaning of this dream is that the slaughtered cattle are my companions who will be martyred; the blade of my sword being broken means one of my family will be killed; and the metal coat of armor signifies Medina.'"

We all fell silent as we thought of the implications of this dream and its interpretation. The Prophet's ﷺ dreams were not like ours—they told of the future. It seemed that if we were to engage in battle again, there would be Martyrs and Medina would be protected, *insha'Allah*.

My father continued, "The Prophet said that his wish was to engage the enemy in a defensive position, only if the Quraysh actually attacked the city. However, there were many present at the meeting who wished to meet them in battle, including the Prophet's uncle, Hamza. After consideration, the Prophet said to us; 'Very well, so make ready for battle! If you are patient, you will again encounter help from Allah.'"

Excitement welled in my chest—another expedition accompanying the Holy Prophet ﷺ! I rushed to prepare myself, and my mother helped me. I could tell she was worried, as any mother would be. She forbade my father from going, as he had been unwell of late. He reluctantly agreed. I gathered my sword, sharpened my knife and checked my arrows. In my enthusiastic preparations, I did not think too much about what the Prophet ﷺ had said regarding patience.

Later at *Jumu`ah*, we sat and listened to the Prophet ﷺ. He told us what a noble deed it was, defending one's home and fighting for the sake of Allah. The way he spoke filled me with such awe. The Prophet ﷺ and a few of his Companions then went to his rooms.

We were all in a state of readiness and excitement. My father and I had been practising the bow and arrow and I was actually quite a skilled shot. I had even shot a lizard, scampering along a rock, half a *ghalwa* away!

"Abdul Karim! Come, I have a gift for you." My father held out a leather quiver for the arrows we had made. He had made it himself in his workshop. He was a leatherworker by trade, making sandals mostly, but also some armor and quivers. I took the quiver and felt the smooth leather, probably camel hide, and admired his workmanship.

"I am sorry I cannot join you in battle, son."

I looked at him and looked away as a tear formed. I had been worried about him. I took a breath. "Don't worry father, I will be okay."

He put his hand on my shoulder. "I know—you are a strong fighter."

We heard the *adhan* and returned to the Mosque to join the `Asr* prayer. After the prayer, some of the leaders of the Ansar were debating amongst themselves about the battle. The Prophet ﷺ came out from his apartment in full armor. He looked an impressive sight, full of nobility and *Allah's* Power.

Someone of the Ansar called out, "O *RasoolAllah*, if our opinion was contrary to your view, we beg your pardon, we will do whatever you say. If you think it is better not to leave the city, we will stay within and defend Medina when attacked."

However, the Prophet ﷺ said, "Nay, for when a prophet of Allah has girded himself for battle to combat the enemy of God, he will never lay down his arms, unless the Command of the Lord comes to him." The Prophet ﷺ then leapt upon his steed and sounded the battle-cry.

All of us grouped together and followed the Prophet ﷺ out of the city. Just as my companions and

I were near the gates of Medina, we saw hundreds of men under `Abdullah bin Ubayd ibn Saul, turning on their heels, and heading back toward Medina. It looked like they were deserting us, fleeing from the battle and our army. How could anyone desert the Holy Prophet? It seemed to us like pure cowardice.

As we were walking along, I recounted stories of the great Battle of Badr to some of the younger boys: Usamah, `Abdullah and Thabit ibn Zaid, most of them not yet fourteen. They hoped if they walked with us and were not noticed, they would be allowed into the army as well, even though they were too young.

The Prophet ﷺ came up to us. I stood to attention and gazed at his Holy Countenance. He said, "We are facing a great battle and it is not the place for children. You will have to turn back from here and go home."

The boys' shoulders fell with disappointment to not be part of this important mission. I felt bad for them. But if the Prophet ﷺ said for them to go, it was for the best. The battlefield would be a dangerous place, they didn't know how brutal it could be.

Some of the older boys were to be selected though. Rafi' bin Hajid drew himself up on his toes to seem taller, as his best friend spoke up: "O RasoolAllah, please don't leave me out! I always throw Rafi when I am wrestling with him, so please let me be in your army too."

The Prophet ﷺ smiled at them. "Alright, show us. Wrestle with your friend and let us see."

They began, and I was impressed with their skills as wrestlers. Afterwards, we looked to the Prophet ﷺ who agreed that they could join us.

There were seven hundred of us in all, mostly men of all ages, with a few warrior women, as well as the women who brought food and medical supplies. I looked back briefly to see if I could see 'Asma, and saw her there in the group, she was chatting with the others. She glanced in my direction and I looked down, feeling a bit shy.

We marched on foot towards the mountain of Uhud across the dry, rocky desert. Our army only had two horses and a few camels. That night I was selected to patrol the outer fringes of our camp, and we climbed atop the hills to gaze out, searching for signs of the enemy. The stars were forming a blanket of light across the sky, as though expectantly watching for whatever may occur.

Later that night, I found a spot to rest, checking the space first for snakes and scorpions. I felt the enemy were like these poisonous creatures,

heading towards us, intent on our defeat and hoping to extinguish the light of Islam. I was not going to let them do that, *insha'Allah*.

The next day, we positioned ourselves in front of the mountain of Uhud. This gave us a good vantage point: we were protected on all sides by the mountain with a small pass to the east. As we lined up, the Prophet ﷺ selected fifty of the best archers, and I was one of them. `Abdullah ibn Jubayri was our commander. We were instructed to defend the pass against a likely attack from behind our lines.

The Prophet ﷺ said to our commander, "Whatever happens to us may happen, whether we lose or win. Unless you receive orders from me, do not under any circumstances leave your position. Even if all the unbelievers are slaughtered and nobody at all is left, if you have no word from me, do not leave your place."

We had our orders, so we waited on top of the hill—a good vantage point. We scanned the horizon...

There! The enemy approached.

As they came into clear view, we saw they were well-equipped: armed to the teeth with cavalry and camels. There were thousands of them. And wasn't that Khalid Ibn Walid travelling on one flank, sitting on a black horse? He was renowned for his strategy in battle, but we felt so invincible that I was sure not even he could harm us today, and there was Ikramah, Abu Jahl's son, on the other. Women called and chanted to the men from behind the army, shouting that they better kill the Muslims so that they could sleep in their beds.

The energy mounted. War drums boomed around the valley. Dust clouds billowed into the air from horse's hooves.

"*Allahu Akbar!*" the Prophet ﷺ shouted.

The rest of us began chanting as loud as we could, "*Allah, Allah, Allah!*"

The power that came from the Prophets' ﷺ cry and the *dhikr* of Allah ﷻ, made the drums seem like nothing. It cast fear into the hearts of the enemy, and made our hearts strong and ready.

The Prophet ﷺ said, "There is no escape from fate, fear cannot deter destiny; to fear the enemy of God is shameful, to confront him is honour and glory!"

Then the Prophet ﷺ drew his engraved sword in front of everyone and asked, "Who will take this sword and give it it's right?"

His Companion, Abu Dujanah ؓ, had the honour of taking this sword.

A renegade from the tribe of Aws stepped out and cried, "O, men of Ansar! I am sure you know me. I am Abu Amir." He waited. He seemed to think some of the Ansar would desert our ranks and join him.

Someone from the Ansar replied, "Oh yes, we know you very well for the impious, corrupt person that you are, but make sure you know this well: the Lord will not fulfil your desires."

The Quraysh then demanded single combat. They sent Talha out, a renowned warrior. The Prophet ﷺ sent ʿAli ؓ to fight him. He finished Talha in a few strokes of his sword.

Talha's son, enraged at seeing his father lying in the dust, came out next, and the Prophet ﷺ sent Hamza ؓ. Again, we were victorious.

Angered, the Quraysh charged forth and the battle began in earnest. We fired our arrows when we had the chance, but we had to ensure there were enough for a possible attack from the rear. We could only look on from our vantage point, frustrated at not being able to join in the fighting, but we had our orders.

The standard of the Makkans passed from man to man as each one was destroyed by our most fierce fighters. Saʿad bin Abu Waqqas ؓ shot an arrow straight at Abu Talha from the Makkans; the standard continued to be passed between no less than seven men in the space of a short time. The smell of sweat and blood filled our nostrils. Their women continued to drum in the background.

ʿAli ibn Abi Talib ؓ fought with such might that it seemed every man of the enemy must have felt his sword. Men seem to fall to the ground with one blow, such was his strength. No wonder the Prophet ﷺ

named both him and Hamza ؓ, the Lions of Allah. They ploughed through the enemy with an unstoppable power.

Finally, the army of the Quraysh retreated. As the Muslims pushed forward, the women at the back of the Makkan army broke ranks and fled. The rest of the men soon followed, leaving all their provisions and possessions on the battleground. Believing they had won, my Muslim brothers lowered their arms and began to collect the booty.

Our commander, ʿAbdullah ibn Uways ؓ said, "There is now no need to guard this pass. Ahead of us is all clear—let us go out into the battlefield."

If we didn't go and claim some of the booty, the others would have all of it. We looked at ʿAbdullah ibn Jabayr ؓ for instruction.

He said, "The Messenger of Allah told us not to leave this place under any circumstances, unless he gave the command!"

It was true the Prophet ﷺ had said that, but our commander had told us to go to the battlefield and we wanted our share of the reward. *It will be fine*, I thought, as I joined the others. Only a few remained on the hill, including my friend, Harith. He shook his head as he looked at me leaving. *I'll get something for him*, I thought to myself. *He'll be glad I went.*

We ran down to the battlefield and started filling our bags with what we could find. Suddenly, shouts echoed over the desert from behind us. I looked up and was horrified to see that our position was being overwhelmed by Khalid ibn Walid and the enemy, having made a surprise rear attack. The helmet I had been stuffing into my bag suddenly felt like ice as I realised what we had done.

The cold feeling of fear stayed with me as I got up and ran towards them. It was too late to help the archers—they had all been killed. I saw Harith lying there, a stab of pain and anguish shot through my heart.

The enemy had now taken full control of an attack at the rear. Enraged, I ran at them, using my sword to attack one soldier and then another, the

Battle of Uhud

Mount Uhud

The Muslim army

50 Muslim archers

Khalid Ibn Walied attack

The Makkan army

Date: 7 Shawwal, 2 AH (625)
Battle duration: 4+ hours
Opponents: Quraysh of Makkah

Number of Muslims: 700
Number of animals: 70 Camels
2 horses

Number of opponents: 3000
Number of animals: 1000 Camels,
200 horses

Muslim martyrs: 62-75
Muslims taken prisoner: 0
Opponent deaths: 22-35
Opponents taken prisoner: 0

100 Infantry

50 Cavalry

100 Camels

غزوة أحد ٧ شوال ٢ هـ

anger pushing my shame away.

I stumbled and fell, and saw Hamza˒ close by, lying on the ground and clutching a spear that had pierced his heart. No! My heart sank as I tried to move towards him, but the enemy stopped me in my tracks. About to receive a fatal blow, I used my shield and warded off the strikes, then began my own attack. I glanced over at Hamza˒ again and I felt nauseous. A slave was cutting out his liver and his ears.

"The Prophet has been killed!" someone shouted from the fray.

My body froze; the fight drained out of me. `Umar˒ stood in the distance with a stunned look on his face. The enemy was gaining power. I had to move, to change position. I ran to the back of the fighting and came upon a group of twelve men fighting valiantly, and in the middle was the Prophet ﷺ. Relief flooded my chest.

I fought off the enemy again as best I could, but many had not seen him. "He's alive! The Prophet has not been killed!" I shouted, but the battle's intensity stole my words. A big oaf kept pushing me in the chest, so I couldn't catch my breath.

Ka'b bin Malik˒ cried out, "O Muslims, here is the Prophet. He is here!"

Unfortunately, the enemy also heard these cries and focused on where he stood. The Muslims were now forming a shield so the Prophet ﷺ would not be hurt. Men were falling, martyred.

Umm Ummara˒, one of our fiercest warrior women, positioned herself between the enemy and

curse against them."

He replied, "I was not sent to curse, but I was sent as a summoner and as a mercy. O Allah, guide my people for they do not know."

Then Umar~ said, "My mother and father be your ransom, O Messenger of Allah! The prophet Noah invoked a curse against his people when he said, '*My Lord, do not leave one of the rejectors upon the Earth.*' (71:26) Had you invoked a curse like that against us, we would have been destroyed to the last man. Your back has been trodden on, your face has been bloodied and your tooth has been broken, and yet you refuse to utter anything but good. You have said, 'O Allah, forgive my people for they do not know.'"

Then, Wahab bin Kabu~ arrived on the battlefield, a noble-looking man. He engaged the enemy in an impressive onslaught, fighting twenty attackers at a time. This pushed the enemy back. Wahab ر fell though; another Martyr heading straight for the Divine Presence.

Even though the enemy almost claimed the better of us, we managed one final push and there was a lull in the fighting. The Prophet ﷺ decided to withdraw. We moved to a more protected part of the mountain and I sat exhausted on a rock. A wound on my arm throbbed. The sun beat down. I chose a place away from the others, not wanting to be seen.

We expected the enemy to scale the mountain, but for some reason they could not manage it. My friend told me it was because the Prophet ﷺ had prayed to Allah for extra support.

Abu Sufyan shouted out from the bottom of the mountain, "Is Muhammad with you?"

The Prophet ﷺ indicated that no one should reply. Abu Sufyan then asked about Abu Bakr~ and ʿAli~ and ʿUmar~...but no one answered.

Abu Sufyan said, "This means to say that they are dead; the backbone of Islam is broken. We have attained our goal; this new religion is extinguished."

the Holy Prophet ﷺ to protect him. She was incredible, fighting off one warrior after the next. But the enemy was so intent, they closed in on him. One of them hit our Holy Prophet ﷺ, and blood poured from his face. Those cursed men were laid to the ground by our fighters. Bits of metal had lodged into the face of the Prophet ﷺ and Abu Ubaydah~ bent over him to remove them with his teeth, damaging his own teeth. The Prophet's ﷺ daughter, Fatima~, came rushing to the battlefield and tried to help her father as the intense battle continued. The Muslims were forced back.

The Companions, on seeing the Prophet ﷺ so badly injured, said, "If only you would invoke a

This was too much for `Umar, who shouted back, "Oh no! You vile and treacherous one, who has declared war on Allah and His Holy Prophet. Go and tell your men that Allah has withered the lips of the one that tries to extinguish this religion! All those whom you ask about are among the living, and they are soldiers of Allah's army. They will come to exact their revenge on you yet."

Abu Sufyan sounded confused when he said, "Well, the fortunes of war are variable. Today we have had our revenge on Badr."

"Nay," replied Umar. "It is not at all like that. In this too, you are in error. For our victory is from the bounty of Allah, while your victory is from the world of the Fire which is the place of purification for the unbelievers."

"O, great Hubal!" said Abu Sufyan, addressing the old Makkan idol, Hubal.

`Umar replied, "There is no God but Allah and Allah is the Most High and Eternal!"

"We have Uzza as well," replied Abu Sufyan.

"And Allah is our Lord."

"O `Umar, is Muhammad still alive?"

"I swear by Allah Almighty that he is listening to all our prattle. That is the truth. Next year we will be back to measure ourselves against you, then you will see how it shall be." (1)

With that, Abu Sufyan left. It seemed the Quraysh had decided to ride back to Makkah.

We followed the Prophet ﷺ back to the battlefield and helped to dig the graves of those who had fallen and the women tended to the wounded. The Prophet ﷺ wandered the field, stopping at each of the dead, gazing down for a while and making prayers. He stopped and prayed for Harith. I knew he was now in a better place. We saw the tears of the Prophet ﷺ fall on those blessed Martyrs. When he came to his beloved uncle, Hamza, he bent down to embrace him. His deep sadness was clear to see.

Later, as we prayed together for the dead, the Holy Prophet ﷺ was overcome many times as we all were. Great sadness lay in our hearts, but we knew the Martyrs had died a most honourable death serving Allah Almighty. They had reached Paradise.

The Holy Prophet ﷺ spoke; "I bear witness that these friends of mine placed their own self-interest last, and that they surrendered their lives and souls in Allah's cause. Yes, in the eternal world to come, on that second Day of Gathering, those who were wounded for the sake of Allah will rise from their graves, blood flowing afresh from their wounds. No man nor angel will at that instance not feel passionate love for the colour of that Martyr's blood, and indeed, will become intoxicated on the scent issuing from it."

An *Ayat* from the Qur'an was revealed about what happens to those who die in Allah's way, which gave comfort to us:

"'And never think of those who have been killed in the cause of Allah as dead. Rather, they are alive with their Lord, receiving provision, rejoicing in what Allah has bestowed upon them of His bounty, and they receive good tidings about those [to be martyred] after them who have not yet joined them— that there will be no fear concerning them, nor will they grieve. They receive good tidings of favor from Allah and bounty and [of the fact] that Allah does not allow the reward of believers to be lost—those [believers] who responded to Allah and the Messenger after injury had struck them. For those who did good among them and feared Allah is a great reward. Those to whom hypocrites said, "Indeed, the people have gathered against you, so fear them." But it [merely] increased them in faith, and they said, "Sufficient for us is Allah, and [He is] the best Disposer of affairs." (Family of Imran; 169-173)

As I stood before the newly filled graves, I could not help but think of the Prophet's ﷺ sadness and the great number who had died. Shame and humiliation flowed through me. We had deserted our Companions on the hill in favour of greed. Harith and Hamza and many other excellent Muslims died because of our bad choice. The Prophet ﷺ had been wounded and in danger of his life. I could not face my friends, my family, and especially the Prophet ﷺ. I felt like the worst traitor, only fit for the rubbish dump, wishing that I had died instead of those noble ones.

My comrades, who had also deserted the hill, wore the same expressions of shame. Some of them, braver than I, approached the Prophet ﷺ to express their deep remorse.

The Prophet ﷺ called everyone together. "Be not overly distraught, for you have been forgiven. The conquest of Makkah is near."

Great relief flooded through me. The Prophet ﷺ said we were forgiven, *alhamdulillah*. I was also relieved to not get a severe punishment for disobeying orders. My heart filled with even more love for our Prophet ﷺ, in whom I could find no fault.

Some *ayats* of Qur'an were revealed to us about our weakness in the battle:

"And Allah had certainly fulfilled His promise to you when you were killing the enemy by His permission until [the time] when you lost courage and fell to disputing about the order [given by the Prophet] and disobeyed after He had shown you that which you love. Among you are some who desire this world, and among you are some who desire the Hereafter. Then he turned you back from them [defeated] that He might test you. And He has already forgiven you, and Allah is the possessor of bounty for the believers." (Family of Imran:152)

"Indeed, those of you who turned back on the day the two armies met, it was Satan who caused them to falter on account of their weakness [for material gains]. But Allah forgave them. Indeed, Allah is Oft-Forgiving and Most Forbearing." (Family of Imran: 155)

We headed back to Medina carrying the wounded, of which there were many. Excruciating pain throbbed in my arm from a deep wound. I was glad to walk in through the front door of my home and fall into my mother's arms. Exhaustion overcame me. I retreated to my bed and she tended my wounds. I didn't feel like talking much.

Shortly after, my father told me that the Prophet ﷺ had set out once again with seventy strong men; joined by another six hundred, and those only lightly wounded. The intention was to pursue the enemy who were bound to return, having almost achieved their goal of wiping us out. However, the Prophet ﷺ returned to Medina soon after he left; it seemed that the enemy chose not to return after all.

Most households that night cried, in grief of those we had lost. I thought sadly of Harith, remembering all the times we'd had. And Hamza, one of the most noble of men, a great warrior and one of the Prophet's ﷺ noble family.

In the morning we heard that the Prophet ﷺ prayed for the enemy who had injured him by the sword. The Prophet ﷺ did not order retaliation for the person who did that to him. Instead, the Prophet ﷺ said, "O Allah, forgive my people for they do not know."

The Prophet ﷺ was so forgiving, and he'd said Allah had forgiven us—the ones who deserted our posts—so why was I still so remorseful?

Then, I remembered the *ayat* from Qur'an:
"And if, when they wronged themselves, they had come to you, [O Muhammad], and asked forgiveness of Allah and the Messenger had asked forgiveness for them, they would have found Allah accepting of repentance and Merciful. (The Women:64)

I had to go and see the Prophet ﷺ himself. During a quiet moment, when the Prophet ﷺ was sitting on his own, I forced myself to approach him. Feeling like the worst person to ever walk the

Earth, I kept my eyes downcast. I could barely look at his face. As he turned, I caught his eye for a split second and he looked at me with such compassion, such love, my eyes filled with tears. I knew then that he had truly forgiven me, and that now I could forgive myself.

"I am sorry, my Prophet."

He smiled, and his words reminded me that we have yet to attain perfection. I remembered what the Prophet ﷺ had told us before battle; "If you are patient, you will again encounter help from Allah."

I saw that day, what it meant to be patient. Even if all the world was crying out to do something, and logic said otherwise, I would never doubt the words of the Prophet ﷺ. That meant having strength on another level, more difficult to come by than fighting a hundred brave warriors on the battlefield.

"And never think of those who have been killed in the cause of Allah as dead. Rather, they are alive with their Lord, receiving provision, Rejoicing in what Allah has bestowed upon them of His bounty, and they receive good tidings about those [to be martyred] after them who have not yet joined them - that there will be no fear concerning them, nor will they grieve. They receive good tidings of favor from Allah and bounty and [of the fact] that Allah does not allow the reward of believers to be lost - Those [believers] who responded to Allah and the Messenger after injury had struck them. For those who did good among them and feared Allah is a great reward - Those to whom hypocrites said, "Indeed, the people have gathered against you, so fear them." But it [merely] increased them in faith, and they said, "Sufficient for us is Allah, and [He is] the best Disposer of affairs."
(Aali Imran 3:169-173)

"And Allah had certainly fulfilled His promise to you when you were killing the enemy by His permission until [the time] when you lost courage and fell to disputing about the order [given by the Prophet] and disobeyed after He had shown you that which you love. Among you are some who desire this world, and among you are some who desire the Hereafter. Then he turned you back from them [defeated] that He might test you. And He has already forgiven you, and Allah is the possessor of bounty for the believers." (Aali Imran 3:152)

"Indeed, those of you who turned back on the day the two armies met, it was Satan who caused them falter on account of their weakness (for material gains). But Allah forgave them. Indeed, Allah is Oft-Forgiving and Most Forbearing." (Aali Imran 3:155)

How Did the Prophet ﷺ Deal with Captives?

Out of a total of 6,565 captives taken over his lifetime, the Prophet Muhammad ﷺ only ordered the execution of two men, and not for being at war with him but for their well-known crimes.

The Prophet ﷺ would be concerned about the captives after a battle and wanted to ensure they were treated fairly.

Although the Companion 'Umar ر sometimes wanted to kill the prisoners for their crimes, the Prophet ﷺ instead asked for ransoms from their families and then released the prisoners. If the family could not afford the ransom, then the Prophet ﷺ, with his compassion, still let the prisoners return to their families without having to pay anything.

We can hear how he treated the slave, Wahshi ر*, who killed his beloved uncle Hadrat Hamza ر. Wahshi later became Muslim. The Prophet ﷺ was pleased but asked his Companions not to bring him in front of him, because seeing him reminded him of the sad day. Most commanders would have ordered his execution for killing a family member.

There was another man, Suhail bin 'Amar ر *, who used to compose terrible verses against the Prophet ﷺ. He was brought as a prisoner of war after the Battle of Badr and Hadrat 'Umar ر suggested to pull his two front teeth out for what he had spoken, but the Prophet ﷺ did not allow even that. The Prophet ﷺ said, to teach the Muslims, *"Allah may disfigure me on the day of Judgement, were I to do so."*

If someone could read and write, then their ransom would be to teach ten Muslims to read and write.

* Why do some people have the honourific symbol ر representing 'radi Allahu 'anhu, may Allah be pleased with them, after their name when they committed crimes or fought against the Prophet ﷺ? This was because eventually these people became Muslim and invariably became ardent supporters of the Prophet ﷺ. When someone enters Islam, all their sins of the past are wiped clean.

CAPTIVES IN THE BATTLE OF BADR

After the Battle of Badr, the captives had been tied to different pillars and one of the captives was the Prophet's ﷺ uncle, 'Abbas bin Muttalib ر, who had reluctantly accompanied the battle. The ropes were too tight and he was moaning in pain. The Prophet ﷺ was disturbed to hear this and began pacing restlessly. The Companions asked why he was so perturbed. The Prophet ﷺ told them what was troubling him and they immediately went to loosen his bonds. The Prophet ﷺ said this can only be done if all the bonds were loosened of all the prisoners, so it was done.

Folio 66A of the Jami al-Tawarikh, from the Khalili Collection, illustrating a scene prior to the Battle of Badr by Rashid al-Din

'Abdullah ibn 'Amr ر reported: The Messenger of Allah ﷺ said; "Those who are merciful will be shown mercy by the Most Merciful. Be merciful to those on the earth and the One in the heavens will have mercy upon you."

(al-Tirmidhi)

The Prophet Muhammad ﷺ said; "Accustom yourselves to do good if people do good, and to not do wrong even if they commit evil."

(al-Tirmidhi)

ORIENTALISM

It is worth mentioning the Orientalists, who spent a great deal of time and energy promoting the idea that Islam was a 'dark' and 'misguided' religion that was merely spread by the sword, and whose influence is still seen today throughout the West.

The Orientalist writers of the 19th century were mostly academic Christian men, who, by proclaiming themselves 'experts' misinformed the West about Islam. Some learnt Arabic and travelled to Muslim lands, and so many did not doubt their viewpoints and accounts.

They were fascinated by Middle Eastern and African cultures but always had a superior attitude, as if the West was rational, flexible and superior, and the East was barbaric and uncultured.

They wrote about the Prophet Muhammad ﷺ in very unfavourable terms, making him out to be war-hungry and only seeking power for himself.

Even with their best efforts to put people off 'the dark religion of Islam', the Historian and Orientalist, William Muir, could not help be impressed at the kindness and compassion shown to prisoners of war by the Prophet ﷺ, as we can read in this account:

"In pursuance of Muhammad's commands, the citizens of Medina, and such of the refugees as possessed houses, received the prisoners, and treated them with much consideration. 'Blessings be on the men of Medina!' said one of these prisoners in later days, 'they made us ride, while they themselves walked: they gave us wheaten bread to eat when there was little of it; contenting themselves with dates.'

It is not surprising that when, some time afterwards, their friends came to ransom them, several of the prisoners who had been thus received declared themselves adherents of Islam...Their kindly treatment was thus prolonged, and left a favourable impression on the minds even of those who did not at once go over to Islam."

William Muir, The Life of Muhammad, 1861

The Orientalists had a fascination with Muslim culture, focusing on the Umayyad, Abbasid and Ottoman dynasties with the sumptuous palaces, the harems and the many conquests. All this, of course, was nothing to do with the example of the Prophet Muhammad ﷺ who based his life on worshipping Allah and building a safe and better society.

A Lady Receiving Visitors, by John Frederick Lewis 19th Century

The Story of the Battle of the Trench

'Abdul Karim continues his acount of the events recorded at the Battle of the Trench from the 5th Shawwal, 5 A.H. (626 C.E.).

We had heard, through the Prophet's ﷺ scouts, that a huge force was being gathered to fight against us. The tribes of the Bani Nadir and the Bani Qaynuqa, who had been expelled from Medina because of their assassination attempt on the Messenger of Allah ﷺ last year, had been meeting with the Quraysh. They had also united with the Ghatafan tribe, the Bani Murra, Bani Asad, the Bani Sulaym, and the tribes of Ashja. It seemed as if the whole of Arabia was pitched against us.

How could they not hear the message of the Prophet ﷺ ? He only brought peace, hope, and mercy. Could they not see that?

Over the last year, the Quraysh had been persecuting us by sending small bands of warriors to attack those who left Medina and I was starting to think it wasn't safe to leave the city. Forty of my father's friends were invited to teach Islam to some of the nearby tribes, and they were all assassinated on the way. I couldn't believe it—all of those men had memorized the Qur'an, they were the guardians of Allah's Words.

My father attended the war meeting with the other elders of the *Ansar*. I wanted to, but I was still too young so I waited outside. Sometime later, the men began to leave. I moved towards them to find out what was happening.

Salman al Farsi appeared at the door. He was different to a lot of us; his pale skin and fine features showed that he was from the north. I had heard he was once a Christian and then a slave. He smiled at me but with a look of concern. "Make haste. We haven't got much time," he said.

I waited until my father appeared and eagerly questioned him. "Father, are we going into battle again?"

"This time is a bit different, my son. Salman has suggested a good plan to the Messenger of Allah who accepted it. We are going to dig a trench across the north-west border of Medina to stop the attack. These are methods used by the great armies of Persia which we hope will grant us success, *insha'Allah*. The Quraysh and whoever has sided

with them could be here in a matter of days, so we must work hard to complete the trench."

A few thousand men and boys were gathered to dig the trench and we were divided into groups of ten. I was so pleased to be placed fairly near the Prophet ﷺ. Each team had to dig a ditch seventy feet long, thirty feet wide and fifteen feet deep around the borders of Medina. The completed trench would be about three miles long.

The ground was hard, rocky, and dry, and it was exhausting work. I paused for a moment, leaning on my shovel, with sweat streaming down my face. I looked over at the Prophet ﷺ. He seemed calm and unruffled and to be working faster than everyone else. He seemed to have the strength of one hundred men, even though he was three times my age.

We kept digging night and day, only resting when we needed to and barely stopping to eat. Sometimes food was passed around, but there was so little food in Medina and we went for whole days without it. We would sing some verses to keep us going:

"We're the ones who've pledged ourselves to Muhammad; we pledged to do jihad for as long as we live."

"The enemy is attacking us to make us leave the truth, but we stubbornly refuse to oblige."

The Prophet ﷺ replied to our verses, saying:

"O Lord! Had You not guided us in Your Grace and Mercy, how sorry would have been our state! We would have not known about worship, nor would we have followed the path of guidance!"

A huge boulder was stopping progress. None of our tools or the strongest men could budge it. The Prophet ﷺ was notified and he came over with his pickaxe. He cried, "*Bismillah ir-Rahman ir-Rahim!*" and struck the rock.

He struck it three times, and each time, a section of the rock broke away. "*Allahu Akbar!*" The Prophet ﷺ exclaimed. "By Allah, at this moment I behold the red roofs of Damascus! Now I see the gates to the city of Sanaa." After another strike, he said, "By Allah, I now behold the white houses of Mada'in belonging to the Khosroes. The arm rings of Khosroes will be slipped onto Saraqa's wrist."

I was told that the Prophet ﷺ was predicting that Islam would spread to all of these lands. I looked around at our men listening to the Prophet ﷺ, and those working hard in the distance. We were

probably gravely outnumbered by the Quraysh, yet the Prophet ﷺ predicted success in the future. It was all in Allah's Hands.

We were making good progress as the days wore on, even though the sun seemed hotter by the day and I could feel my strength dwindling. '*Bismillah ir-Rahman ir-Rahim*!' I would say to myself to keep going, and it always gave me the extra strength I needed.

Amazingly, we finished within twenty days, with Allah's Support. The trench was huge, stretching out in either direction, forming a protective barrier. How were we going to get out afterwards? Our city was now cut off from the rest of the world.

It turned out that we had finished it just in time. The very next day we heard from the scouts that a huge army was approaching. They estimated ten thousand men. The women and children were sent to the far corners of the city for safety while we prepared for a defensive battle. Again, we were outnumbered by over three men to one.

The first few enemy riders cantered up on their horses. Because we did not meet them for battle, they confidently rode up towards the gates of Medina as if to claim victory—that is, until they spotted the huge trench. Confusion appeared on their faces as they looked beyond the trench and saw our archers' arrows trained on them. They swiftly turned around to rejoin their men and we watched them gallop away. They had no choice but to set up camp, and probably had little preparations for one. *Insha'Allah*, we hoped they would not last long.

We were well-defended behind the large mounds of earth, with plenty of rocks on hand in case they tried to cross the trench. We also had our archers, including myself, at the ready.

Meanwhile, there were whispers among our ranks that the Bani Qurayza - a Jewish tribe who lived in Medina and who had signed a peace contract with the Prophet - had secretly sided with the enemy. This was unnerving as their fort

was located behind us, inside Medina, near to where the women and children were. We could not leave our post long enough to go and interrogate the Bani Qurayza. We just had to hope it was not true. Some of our men went to check on them and everyone seemed safe, at least for the time being.

We waited all night, lined up along the trench, taking turns to rest while others kept watch. We had to be vigilant—there were several miles of the trench to watch and we couldn't take our eyes off it for a moment.

At first light, we heard shouts as the enemy attacked; arrows rained down on us and we fired back in return. They began to try and cross the trench with no success. The enemy's huge number was threatening - we would be easy targets if they managed to get across.

Salman's trench seemed to be working: none of the enemy soldiers succeeded in crossing. They could have stretched themselves out across the whole line of our trench and attacked all at once, but they knew this was too great a risk because we Muslims had superior hand-to-hand battle skills and they would have suffered a great loss.

The siege had now lasted for twenty days. Watchmen were needed all day and all night and I could see the exhaustion and the weariness on my brothers' faces. *Insha'Allah*, Allah would send the strength we needed. The rumors about the Bani Qurayz, the lack of sleep, and the scarcity of food were taking its toll on our army. There were days when we could not even stop for five minutes to say our prayers. There was fear everywhere. I felt myself exhausted to the point of fainting. I looked towards the Prophet ﷺ—he was always so composed, unworried, relying completely on Allah. My heart filled with strength once again, just looking at His Holy face.

"Abdul Karim!"

I heard 'Asma's voice. I turned and saw her and some others arriving with some much-needed water and food for the men. She looked at me shyly, with concern. She could see how hard it was. "How are you?" she asked.

"*Alhamdulillah*, with the Prophet at our side, we are well," I replied bravely.

She smiled and passed me some bread and a cup of water and I smiled back. When she was around I felt so peaceful. I looked towards the Prophet ﷺ who saw us and also smiled. *InshaAllah*, one day, when this was all over, I planned to ask to her to marry me.

The Prophet ﷺ would position himself in the most dangerous areas, and he was concerned about us—the Ansar, and our beloved city—being under attack for embracing this new religion. But our leaders reassured the Prophet ﷺ that what he had brought us was worth more than all the diamonds in the world.

Day after day, the siege continued until at last—frustrated at their lack of success—the enemy decided to send their fiercest warriors on horseback across the trench. First, was the famous 'Amr ibn 'Abdu Wudd, an old but fearless warrior. It was said he had vowed not to wash or comb his hair until Badr was avenged. I was glad I didn't have to share a tent with him! Behind him came Umar Ibn Khattab's ؓ brother, Dirar, then Hubayra bin Abi Wahb, and Ikrama ibn Abu Jahl.

'Amr ibn 'Abdu Wudd shouted out, "Where are you who started this business of *La ilaha il Allah*? Who wishes to destroy all inherited tradition by this claim of One God only, and resurrection after death? I have come and I am ready! I challenge you to send me a man who will fight me. Send out one of your fighters!"

The noble Companions were unsure who they would send out.

'Ali ؓ stepped forward. "I will go!" he said.

The Prophet ﷺ was initially reluctant to agree. But insults were being thrown at the

Prophet ﷺ and 'Ali رضي could stand it no more. He stood up and said, "At least let me prove I am his equal!"

The Prophet ﷺ then placed his own armor on 'Ali and gave him his sword, *Dhul Fiqar*. I would have gone myself, of course, but Ali رضي was a stronger fighter than I was. If I were to fail, the enemy would have felt encouraged. The Prophet ﷺ prayed for 'Ali, then kissed him on his head.

As 'Ali moved forward on foot, 'Amr approached him on horseback. We all wondered at the obvious inequality between the two. 'Amr liked to give his opponents three wishes so he demanded these from 'Ali.

'Ali replied: "That you may come to reason and accept Islam!"

"What?!" roared 'Amr. "You still persist in asking me this?"

"What else do have I to persist in?" 'Ali replied.

'Amr jumped down from his horse and cut the animal with his sword, to the shock of those watching. Then he rushed at 'Ali with his sword raised and struck out, cleaving 'Ali's shield in two. 'Ali drew *Dhul Fiqar* from its sheath and, crying, "*Allahu Akbar!*" he struck 'Amr with such a blow that he fell down dead.

We all cheered; one of their best fighters was down.

Munabbih stepped out from the enemy lines and was met by Zubayr, who killed him, again with one stroke. Then others from the enemy's side came

out: Umar's brother and Abu Jahl's son: Ikrama and Khubayr Abu Wahab. When 'Ali and Zubayr met them to fight, the enemy's best warriors then turned and fled back to their camp. 'Ali and Zubayr could have gone after them, but these were against Ali's principles: he never pursued a fleeing enemy. Angry at the humiliating loss of some of their greatest fighters, the enemy barraged us with a new rain of arrows.

The next day we heard that the Bani Qurayza Jews had indeed betrayed us. They decided to attack near the women's quarters, but Safiya bint Abu Muttalib and the other women fought off the traitors, hitting them with tent poles. They retreated back into their fort.

The Prophet ﷺ prayed to Allah: "O my Lord, do not test this band of Muslims who assert Your Oneness with overly hard trials! They will never turn away from You, so don't expose their faces to the enemy's arrows for much longer!"

The Prophet ﷺ continued to pray: "O Lord! Please send Your Divine Support to this small band of Muslims who believe in Your Unity. If it is Your Will, send against their foes an angelic army, or turn the elements of nature that obey Your Command against the enemy. Fulfill Your promise to me, however You choose to do that!" He then turned to us and said, "The enemy may do whatever he likes, the Lord Almighty is on our side!"

Just as he spoke, a wind started to blow; initially, it was light but it soon became so fierce that we had to kneel and keep low to the ground. I saw the enemy across the trench, backing away with their arms up to protect their faces from the wind and the sand. As the wind grew more powerful, they stumbled and fell. I could just make out their outline through the sand-filled air, crawling towards their camp and their horses. Eventually, it became impossible to see anything at all.

As the wind subsided and the sand settled, we looked across the trench - the enemy was nowhere to be seen.

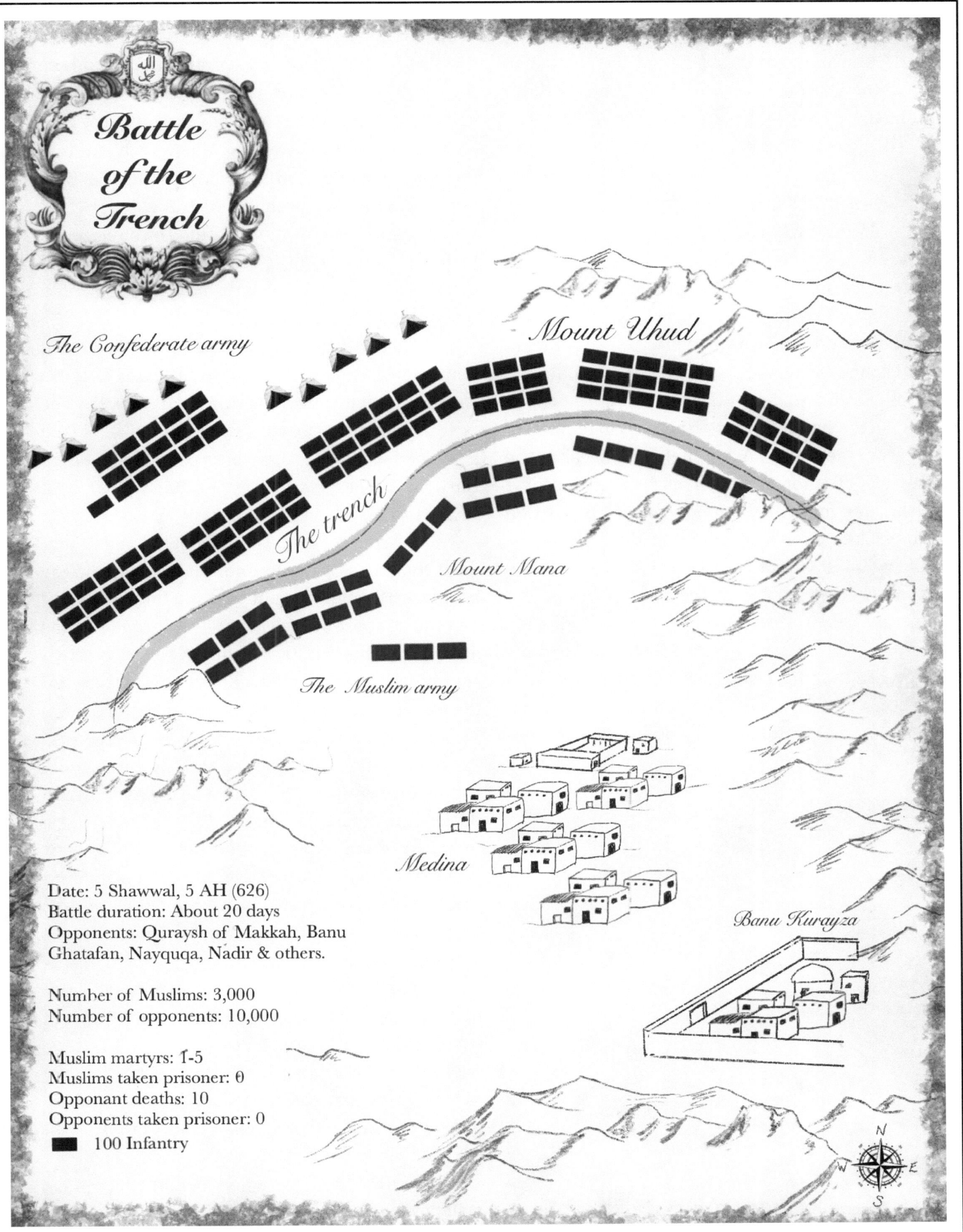

Battle of the Trench

The Confederate army

Mount Uhud

The trench

Mount Mana

The Muslim army

Medina

Banu Kurayza

Date: 5 Shawwal, 5 AH (626)
Battle duration: About 20 days
Opponents: Quraysh of Makkah, Banu Ghatafan, Nayquqa, Nadir & others.

Number of Muslims: 3,000
Number of opponents: 10,000

Muslim martyrs: 1-5
Muslims taken prisoner: 0
Opponent deaths: 10
Opponents taken prisoner: 0

■ 100 Infantry

Hudhayfa bin Yamam was sent to check the situation. When he returned, he said he'd spoken to six unknown men on horseback who said, "O Hudhayfa, go and tell your friend that Allah has turned against his enemies to destroy them." The Prophet ﷺ smiled very broadly and told us that they were, in fact, angels sent by Allah.

Allahu Akbar! Allah had saved us from an army ten times our size. We assessed our casualties which were only five. One of the five was the noble companion Sa'd ibn Mu'adh who had received serious wounds and was moved to a special tent in the Prophet's Mosque where the Prophet ﷺ himself tended to him.

He heard about how Nuaym, an important man from the tribe of Ashja', helped to weaken the resolve of the enemy. Nuaym had secretly become Muslim and thought about how to use his position amongst the enemy to help win the war for us. Nuaym first went to the Bani Qurayza, who had just betrayed us, and told them the Quraysh and Ghatafan tribes were about to give up and leave them to the hands of the Muslims. Nuaym suggested that, for security, they should demand that some of the Quraysh and Ghatafan should join their side as reinforcements and proof of their commitment to battle. The Bani Qurayza agreed this was the best course of action as they could see the siege was wearing thin for the Confederate enemy, whose supplies and morale were very low.

Nuaym then went to Abu Sufyan and told them he had just had a meeting with the Bani Qurayza, who had reunited with the Prophet ﷺ and made a secret treaty with him. To convince the Prophet ﷺ of their loyalty, he said they had promised to give him some hostages from the Quraysh and Ghatafan tribes.

Abu Sufyan was alarmed at this news and immediately sent a message to the Bani Qurayza suggesting that they must join them in battle the next day as their supplies were running low and they needed to strike as soon as possible. The Bani Qurayza agreed, but only if Abu Sufyan sent seventy of his men as hostages.

Of course, Abu Sufyan now thought that what Nuaym said was true and refused to send the hostages. He told the Bani Qurayza they no longer had the support of the Quraysh—let the Muslims deal with them. The relations between them completely broke down and the Bani Qurayza left the battleground and retreated to their fort.

I am sure that they bitterly regretted that they had broken their treaty with us, having lost the alliance with the Quraysh. The treaty between the Jews of Medina and the Muslims had been there to ensure mutual cooperation between us. Their treachery might have cost us the battle. I wondered what the Prophet ﷺ would command us to do... The crime of breaking a treaty by treachery was very serious.

The Prophet ﷺ received a command from Allah to go and deal with the Bani Qurayza straightaway. We marched over to their quarters, without even changing our battle dress.

On the way, the Prophet ﷺ said, "Should the Bani Qurayza show any sign of regret then I will pray for Allah to forgive them."

I knew the Prophet ﷺ would show great leniency, as he always had in the past. Hopefully, they would show regret and ask for forgiveness.

We watched 'Ali go up to the gates of the fort and the Bani Qurayza shouting things at him. 'Ali returned, an angry look upon his face and told us they only said terrible things about the Prophet ﷺ. It was decided that we would lay siege to their fort.

The siege lasted for twenty days. Finally, a Bani Qurayza representative came out and declared that they would accept the judgment of Sa'd ibn Mu'adh as there was a long-term pact between his tribe and the Bani Qurayza. He had been badly injured but gave the verdict that the men-at-arms should be killed and the women and children be given as captives and their belongings confiscated. This followed the laws of the Torah.

If only they had sought pardon from the Prophet ﷺ himself, a much lighter sentence would have been passed. The Prophet ﷺ always forgave. That was a very hard day for all of us. This *ayat* from the Qur'an was revealed about this tragic event:

A Persian miniature depicting the encounter in the Trench.

"Behold! They came on you from above you and from below you, and behold, the eyes became dim and the hearts gaped up to the throats, and ye imagined various [vain] thoughts about Allah! In that situation the Believers were tried: they were shaken as by a tremendous shaking. And behold! The Hypocrites and those in whose hearts is a disease [even] say: 'Allah and His Messenger promised us nothing but delusion!' Behold! A party among them said: 'Oh men of Yathrib! Ye cannot stand [the attack]! therefore go back!' And a band of them ask for leave of Muhammad, saying, 'Truly our houses are bare and exposed,' though they were not exposed they intended nothing but to run away. And if an entry had been affected to them from the sides [of the city], and they had been incited to sedition, they would certainly have brought it to pass, with none but a brief delay! ... They think that the Confederates have not withdrawn; and if the Confederates should come [again], they would wish they were in the deserts [wandering] among the Bedouins, and seeking news about you [from a safe distance]; and if they were in your midst, they would fight but little... When the Believers saw the Confederate forces, they said: 'This is what Allah and his Messenger had promised us, and Allah and His Messenger told us what was true.' And it only added to their faith and their zeal in obedience."* (The Confederates:10-22)

The Prophet Muhammad's ﷺ Weapons and Armour

The Prophet ﷺ owned various pieces of weapons and armour throughout his life. He always liked to give names to objects and each item had its own name as well as pets and animals that he would know.

The Prophet's ﷺ shields were known as az-Zulluq and al-Futaq. There is an account that al-Futaq was given as a gift but had a picture of a statue on it. The Prophet ﷺ did not like images of statues, so he put his blessed hand over it and the picture faded away.

The Prophet ﷺ owned five spears: al-Muthwi, al-Muthni, a lance called an-Nab'ah, a bigger lance called al-Bayda', and a short lance, like a staff, called 'Anazah, which he held while attending the 'Eid festivals, and used to place in front of him to demarcate the area in front of him when he led the prayer. Sometimes, the Prophet walked while holding 'Anazah.

The Prophet ﷺ had a helmet made of iron called al-Muwashah – which was adorned with copper – and another helmet, called as-Sabugh, or Dhu as-Sabugh.

The Prophet Muhammad ﷺ also owned three long shirts, which he would wear in battle. One of them was said to be made of fine green silk brocade. Usually, silk is not permitted for men to wear, although according to a hadith by Ahmad, during battle it is permissible.

There was a quiver called al-Kafur, and a strap for it made from tanned skin, as well as three silver circular rings, a buckle, and an edge made of silver.

The Prophet ﷺ also had a baton called al-'Arjun, and a staff called al-Mamshuq. It is said that this is the same staff that the khulafa' succeeding the Prophet used to hold in their hands.

In total, over his life, he owned nine swords, a quiver, six bows, five spears, seven pieces of armour, two helmets, one of which was made from iron and copper and several shields.

The Prophet Muhammads ﷺ bow and the swords al-Qadib and al-Ma'thur are on display at the Topkapi Palace in Istanbul. The bow is made of bamboo and the case was made by Sultan Ahmad I (1603-1617)

SWORDS OF THE PROPHET ﷺ

AL-QADIB

This sword is one metre long, with gold floral designs and a scabbard of dyed animal hide. A thin-bladed sword that was used more for defence or companionship, when travelling. Written on the side in silver is the inscription, "There is no God but God, Muhammad is the Messenger of God – Muhammad b. 'Abdallah b. 'Abn al-Muttalib". It stayed in the house of the Prophet ﷺ and later was used by the Fatimid khalifs. Now it is displayed at the Topkapi Palace in Istanbul.

AL-MA'THUR

Almost one metre long, with the hilt and cross gilded and studded with rubies and turquoise. This sword was given to 'Abdullah by his father Abdul Muttalib, as a young man and is inscribed, 'Abdulllah b. 'Abd al-Muttalib (his father's name). This was given to the Prophet ﷺ before he received his first revelation.

The Prophet ﷺ brought this sword with him on the migration from Makkah to Medina.

The Prophet ﷺ then gave it to 'Ali ibn Talib ر, his son in law, the fourth Khalif.

ZULFIQAR

This legendary, two bladed sword was given to Sayyidina 'Ali ر by the Prophet ﷺ in the Battle of Uhud and other battles. 'Ali ر used it so effectively that (later) a well-known saying came up: "There is no hero and man like 'Ali - there is no sword like Zulfiqar". The original no longer exists but is said to have been scissor-like as this flag depicts.

A Chinese Muslim flag with the Zulfiqar and 'Ali represented as a lion (dated to the late 18th or the 19th century)

SWORD OF THE PROPHETS

The Prophet ﷺ also owned the "Sword of the Prophets". This is the sword of Prophet Dawud (King David). It is 101 cm in length and made with a silver pommel and iron crossguard. There is an engraving of a man holding a human head in one hand and the sword in another, symbolising the story of David and Goliath. Also engraved are the names of the prophets David, Soloman, Moses, Aaron, Joshua, Zachariah, John, Jesus *(peace and blessings be upon them all)* and Muhammad ﷺ. It is said that the sword will one day be in the hands of al-Mahdi عليه السلام, who is foretold to appear as a saviour in the trials of Armaggedon.

The Muslim Army

Before Islam, Arab warriors were known to be fierce with excellent sword fighting and hand-to-hand combat skills. Their armies were very unorganised, and were more like a mob than an army. They would wear anything they had, and bring whatever weapons they owned. The tribal chief might hand out weapons to those without. They did have some codes of conduct that they followed, and codes of honour were very important. For instance, one, two or three warriors would be chosen at the beginning from each side, for a hand-to-hand duel. Insults could also be exchanged, sometimes in poetry.

There were no ranks in the Arab armies. Commanders were chosen at the start of the battle depending on their skill, bravery or influence over their tribe. If they were victorious, Arabs followed the commands of the general and took their share of the booty such as weapons and supplies after a battle ended. Pre-Islam, the tribes would also pillage and mutilate the dead.

In the early days of Islam, the Prophet Muhammad ﷺ instigated some new rules and structure to the army. He introduced five divisions – central, front, back, left and right. He set out the rules of conduct (see page 61) so that soldiers were not allowed to pillage, rape, or torture and not allowed to mutilate the dead. The soldiers were registered when joining and no underage boys were allowed. The age of joining was possibly around 18 years old. Men who had commitments at home, such as looking after an elderly mother, were discouraged to go. There was no punishment for deserting the army, as it was completely voluntary. The booty was fairly distributed for all who took part.

THE RASHIDUN KHALIFATE

Eventually, in 636, during the Rashidun Khalifate under Hadrat 'Umar ﺭ, soldiers were given a wage and became a trained, professional army.

In the first century of Islam, the Muslim armies had unparalleled success. They were able to defeat the well equipped and experienced armies of the Byzantine and Persian Empires with victory after victory. With the spoils they were able to progressively upgrade their weapons.

Their strengths included being able to navigate and survive in the desert regions, which were impassable for many armies due to extreme heat, and a lack of water and food. The Arabs were hardy people used to the difficulties of desert life. They could survive on dates, camel milk and water for a long time, unlike the other armies who were used to a more varied diet. Often foreign armies had huge

An Arabian army. In the early days they had fewer horses and more camels and not as many flags.

chains of men to deliver and keep supplies to the army and they also needed to protect the large number of civilians who assisted the army. The Muslims did not need to rely on a supply chain.

UNIFORM

The early Muslims came as they wanted, there was no formal uniform. They brought with them whatever weapons and armour they owned. Armour in those days was often made of leather with some chainmail and wooden or metal shields. Many were skilled bowmen.

They wore turbans which were ideal for the desert climate.

A Rashidun (7th century) soldier wearing an iron-bronze helmet, a chainmail hauberk, and leather lamellar armour. His sword hung from a baldric, and he carries a leather shield.

Women sometimes accompanied the Prophet ﷺ into battle.

FEMALE SOLDIERS

The Shar'iah states that women can fight and that it is obligatory to fight if the enemy has surrounded the Muslims. If she fears capture and knows that an indecent assault will be made on her person, she cannot surrender and is obliged to fight.

There were some excellent examples of women fighters in the Prophet's ﷺ army. Arab women are known to be strong, outspoken and a force to be reckoned with. While many traditional Arabian women chose to look after the family and the home, some would also join the Prophet ﷺ on the battlefield.

Um `Ateyya ﺭ tells us, "I went on seven military expeditions with the Prophet ﷺ; I would guard the fighters, provisions, make their food, treat the injured and nurse the ill ones." (Muslim)

Imam Ahmad recalls, six believing women were in the army that besieged Khaibar, their task being to hand arrows to the fighters, prepare food, procure water, treat the wounded, spin yarn and help in (the promotion of) the cause of Allah. Eventually, the Prophet ﷺ allocated shares in the spoils to them. (Ahmad, Abu Dawud)

Umm Ummara Nasba bint Ka'b ﺭ, as we heard in the story of the Battle of Uhud, bravely defended the Prophet ﷺ fighting off the Quraysh and was of such effect as to make the Prophet ﷺ say, "Her manner excelled that of such and such people."

On the day of the Battle of Hunayn, Um Salum ﺭ, for her part, kept a dagger to stab any enemies who would come within her reach. This story is told again by her son Anas, "On the Day of Hunayn, Um Salum had a dagger; when she was seen by her husband, Abu Talha, he told the Prophet, the Messenger of Allah, 'Um Salum is keeping a dagger with her'. When the Prophet ﷺ asked her about it she answered, 'It is to stab the abdomen of any of the Pagans who might come near me.' At which the Prophet laughed." (Muslim)

There are also famous fighters like Khawlah Bint Al-Azwar ﺭ, who was in Khalid ibn Walid's ﺭ army, who amazed her fellow soldiers with her fighting, killing many of the enemy and escaping capture as we will see in later chapters.

THE BEST JIHAD FOR WOMEN

One day, the Prophet's ﷺ wife, 'Aisha ﺭ specifically asked the Prophet ﷺ about Jihad for women, as she had heard him so often say about the high rewards in Paradise. *"I said, 'O Allah's Apostle! Shouldn't we participate in holy battles and Jihad along with you?' He replied, 'The best and the most superior Jihad (for women) is Hajj which is accepted by Allah.' Aisha added: 'Ever since I heard that from Allah's Apostle I have determined not to miss Hajj."(al-Bukhari)*

The Prophet Muhammad ﷺ as Army Commander

"Warfare is ordained for you, though it may be hateful unto you; but it may happen that you hate a thing which is good for you, and it may happen that you love a thing which is bad for you. Allah knows and you know not." (Al-Baqara 2:216)

The Qur'an Ayah indicated that of course, the Prophet ﷺ, who was sent as a mercy to all the worlds and did not even like to harm an ant, was naturally averse to warfare as he did not like to hurt anyone. The Prophet ﷺ was someone who forgave those who even killed his own family, and would never pray for the demise of a people or person when they had wronged him.

But when the command came to fight, the Prophet ﷺ was the first to put on his armour and mount his horse and was the most valiant of all the men.

Imagine being a soldier in an army whose leader led with wisdom, compassion and mercy. You would feel safe that good and wise decisions were being made, you could even in times of peace ask this leader a personal question if you needed to and you would be given his time and attention.

Imagine a leader where time after time you saw such just action that the critical mind could find no error, the heart would fill with love and happiness at the supreme honour of assisting such a noble person in the cause of justice and peace.

Witnessing many battles being won, against seemingly insurmountable odds, you would truly feel that Allah was on your side.

You witness the kind treatment of prisoners - never before seen, the fair distribution of war booty, giving to the poor and the needy while the Prophet ﷺ himself gave everything away to those less fortunate. How often has there been a leader of an army with these characteristics?

The Holy Prophet ﷺ took part in twenty-seven (or some sources say twenty-nine) battles. He fought in eight battles but did not kill anyone. (Except for Ubayy bin Khalaf who died although the Prophet only lightly wounded him).

Noble

Brave

Generous

Patient

Merciful

Wise

Truthful

Kind

THE BRAVERY OF THE PROPHET MUHAMMAD ﷺ

Prophet Muhammad ﷺ was recorded as the bravest person; such was his trust in God. Among many powerful warriors, he was known to be the bravest of them all. One of his companions, Al-Baraa ibn Aazib ر, said:

"WaAllahi, if the war became severe we would shield ourselves from the enemy, by getting behind the Prophet ﷺ and the brave one from amongst us was the one who would stand next to the Messenger of Allah." (Muslim)

Prophet Muhammad ﷺ was quick at facing danger. *"One night, the people of Medina heard a strange noise, which frightened them. Some people set forth in the direction of the sound when they saw the Messenger of Allah ﷺ, already on his way back after having investigated the source of the noise. He was riding an unsaddled horse belonging to Abu Talhah, may Allah be pleased with him, and a sword was hanging around his neck, and he was saying, 'Do not be afraid! Do not be afraid!'"* (al-Bukhari and Muslim)

NON-MUSLIM VIEWS OF THE PROPHET MUHAMMAD ﷺ AS A LEADER

"He was Caesar and Pope in one; but he was Pope without the pretensions, and Caesar without the legions of Caesar. Without a standing army, without a bodyguard, without a palace, without a fixed revenue, if ever a man had the right to say that he ruled by Divine right, it was Muhammad; for he had all the power without its instruments and without its supports."

(Rev. Bosworth Smith, an American Protestant Episcopal Bishop.)

"…I became more than ever convinced that it was not the sword that won the place for Islam in those days in the scheme of life. It was the rigid simplicity, the utter self-effacement of the Prophet, the scrupulous regard for pledges, his intense devotion to his friends and followers, his intrepidity, his fearlessness, his absolute trust in God and in his mission. These and not the sword carried everything before them and surmounted every obstacle."

(Mahatma Gandhi)

THE MOST SUCCESSUL LEADER IN ALL OF HISTORY?

Muslim and non-Muslim historians agree that there has not been, in all of history, a more successful leader. Within ten years, under the command of the Holy Prophet ﷺ, all of Arabia was united. The Muslims won almost all battles against armies three times their size and who were much better equipped. This was achieved with very few casualties even though the enemy was highly aggressive.

Key factors in the success of the Prophet ﷺ:

 **SOUGHT COUNSEL**

He was a master tactician and general, as we hear in the accounts of the battles, but he would also seek counsel from his Companions to see what was the best course of action.

TOTAL ALLEGIANCE FROM HIS TROOPS

The Prophet ﷺ had the complete allegiance and obedience of all his close Companions - they would die for him without a moment's hesitation, such was their love. The Prophet ﷺ always was kind and fair to his army.

GATHER INTELLIGENCE

He would send scouts and have intelligence units that would inform him of the aggressor's movements and plans.

DIPLOMACY

FOLLOWED HEAVENLY GUIDANCE

GOOD TREATMENT OF CAPTIVES

He ordered captives to be well treated or send them home. Many captives became Muslim after the good treatment they received.

FAIR DISTRIBUTION OF WAR BOOTY

All men who fought in the battle would have equal rights to the war booty.

NO CONSCRIPTION

There was no conscription or under-age soldiers and men who had many duties at home, such as caring for their parents would be asked to stay at home. This meant there was goodwill among the men.

The Jewish Tribes

There has always been a lot of focus on the relationship between the Muslims and the Jewish tribes of Medina. The Prophet's intention was always to live with others, including those of different faiths, in peace and good neighbourliness, however when they broke treaties and promises, action needed to be taken.

When Muhammad ﷺ arrived in Medina in 621, there were nine Jewish tribes living there. The Jewish tribes were generally traders, money lenders and farmers.

The Jews were not altogether happy that a new leader of Medina had arrived. This leader also introduced new laws that banned some of their trade such as money lending with high interest rates.

All the Jewish tribes willingly signed the Constitution of Medina (see appendix III) which protected their rights but also prohibited them making alliances with the Quraysh or others who were against the Prophet ﷺ.

BANU NADIR

After the Battle of Badr, in 4 A.H., the chief of the Banu Nadir, Ka'b ibn al-Ashraf, went to the Quraysh and incited them to take up arms once again. He was also a poet who insulted the Muslims and their women in offensive verse. This contravened the Treaty and so the Prophet ﷺ sent a small group to deal with him. He was assassinated and the Jews were frightened at this, although none other was harmed.

The Banu Nadir however continued to incite other tribes against the Prophet ﷺ and plotted to assassinate him at a religious debate that they invited him to. He was informed about their plan when he was walking to the meeting so avoided their plot.

The Prophet ﷺ besieged the fortress and ordered the Banu Nadir to surrender. They held out for fourteen days under promises of assistance from the Banu Qurayza. But when the Banu Qurayza did not show up, they surrendered and left the fortress. The Prophet ﷺ allowed them to carry what they could on camels, except for weapons. They came out dressed in splendour and fine silks, the other Medinites, who were quite poor, were astounded.

Most of them went to Khaybar and ruled over the other inhabitants and some went to Syria. The Prophet ﷺ divided their lands amongst the migrated Muslims from Makkah, the Muhajirun.

BANU QURAYZA

As we read in the story of the Battle of the Trench, the Banu Qurayza were caught attempting to attack the Muslim army from the rear, directly opposing the Constitution and committing an act of outright treachery.

After the battle finished, the Prophet ﷺ went directly to their fort, hoping they would express some remorse so that they could have been shown leniency, but they continued to insult the Prophet ﷺ and showed no regret for their treachery. The Muslims then laid siege to their fort and the Banu Qurayza ultimately surrendered, requesting for Sa'd bin Mu'adh, the chief of the tribe of Aws, to pronounce their punishment according to their own Jewish laws. Therefore, unfortunately, as the Jewish law specified, the men had to be executed and the women and children enslaved. If they had appealed to the Prophet ﷺ, they would have received a much lighter sentence.

A painting of the submission of Banu Nadir to the Muslim troops

BANU QAYNUQA

The Banu Qaynuqa were a tribe of Jews living in Medina who specialised in trading and making jewellery. They began to cause trouble after the Battle of Badr, taunting and jeering at the Muslims and intimidating the Muslim women. They were eventually expelled from Medina after breaking the Constitution of Medina, when one of them tied a Muslim woman's clothes so that they fell off her when she tried to move. The man was then killed by a Muslim because of this. Then a group of the Banu Qaynuqa killed the Muslim man, escalating a whole string of revenge killings. The Prophet ﷺ decided to lay siege to their fortress and the Banu Qaynuqa surrendered and were ordered to leave Medina.

Battle of Khaybar

628 (7 A.H.)

Khaybar was an oasis where there were a number of Jewish forts and habitations. The Jews who lived there were wealthy, with large stores of weaponry as well as cloth and other luxury goods.

After the Banu Nadir were exiled from Medina in 625, they settled at Khaybar. From there they made many plots against the Muslims, instigating the Quraysh and Arabian tribes to attack at the Battle of the Trench, bribing tribes to join them. They also convinced the Banu Qurayza to betray their pact that had been agreed by signing the Constitution of Medina. The Banu Nadir continued to incite tribes against the Prophet ﷺ so it was decided that they had to be dealt with.

The Prophet ﷺ set off with 1,400-1,800 men and some women. These were small numbers compared to the Khaybarian who numbered almost 10,000. However, the Prophet's ﷺ army was able to cover the distance in a very short time, only three days, surprising the enemy who had, as yet, made no preparations.

The forts were besieged. Both sides suffered from a lack of provisions, with Khaybar being very short of water and the Muslims short of food.

The Muslims then besieged the largest and final fort. Several attempts were made to capture this citadel. The first was made by Abu Bakr ﻝ who took the banner and fought, but was unsuccessful. 'Umar ﻝ then charged ahead and fought more vigorously than Abu Bakr ﻝ, but still failed. That night Muhammad ﷺ proclaimed;

"By God, tomorrow I shall give it [the banner] to a man who loves God and His Messenger, whom God and His Messenger love. Allah will bestow victory upon him."

That morning, the Muslims were wondering who should have the honour to carry the banner. When the Prophet ﷺ arrived, he called out to 'Ali ibn Talib ﻝ. All this time, Hadrat 'Ali ﻝ was ill and could not participate in the battles. 'Ali ﻝ came to the Prophet ﷺ, who cured him of his ophthalmia, a painful inflammation, by applying his saliva to 'Ali's ﻝ eyes. The Prophet ﷺ sent him with his flag and 'Ali ﻝ, with new vigour, set out to meet the enemy, bearing the banner of Muhammad ﷺ. When he got near the fort, the garrison came out and he fought them. During the battle, a Jew struck him so that his shield fell from his hand and was lost. In need of a substitute, he picked up the door of the fort and used it to defend himself. The door was said to be so heavy that it took eight men to replace it on its hinges. The Prophet ﷺ thereafter bestowed upon 'Ali ﻝ the name, 'Lion of Allah'.

The two remaining and largest forts then surrendered and the Prophet ﷺ dealt very leniently with them, as was his nature. No one was killed and the inhabitants were allowed to keep their possessions.

The Jews at Khaybar however, who were responsible for the treachery, were told to evacuate and to surrender their wealth. The Jews then asked if they could stay at the oasis and give fifty percent of their crops to the Muslims. The Prophet ﷺ agreed but warned they could be expelled at any time if they breached the truce between them.

This was a great success for the Muslims, with many nearby tribes coming into the fold of Islam.

Number of Muslims: 1,600
Number of Khaybar and Ghatafan: 14,000
Muslim losses: About 20
Khaybar and Ghatafan losses: 93

THE TREATY OF HUDAIBIYYAH

The Treaty of Hudaibiyyah had been signed in 6 A.H. (628) when the Prophet ﷺ tried to enter Makkah to perform Hajj with the Muslims but were prevented by the Quraysh.

Both parties agreed to a pact to de-escalate tensions between the Quraysh and the Muslims in Medina.

It meant that there would be peace for ten years as long as neither side broke the treaty.

The Conditions:

1. The Messenger of Allah will have to return to Medina instead of having entered Makkah that year. The Muslims shall perform their pilgrimage in the upcoming year and they would stay in peace at Makkah for three days including the years onward with no arms except sheathed swords.

2. There will be a truce between both parties for ten years, whereby during this period all the people may enjoy safety and harmony.

3. Whoever wishes to enter into a covenant with the Prophet will be allowed to do so, and whoever wishes to enter into a covenant with the Quraysh will be allowed to do so. Whoever enters into any one of the parties will be considered part of that party. Likewise, any sort of aggression on them will be considered an aggression against that party.

4. Whoever flees to Muhammad from Makkah without the permission of his guardians will be sent back to the Quraysh, but whoever comes to the Quraysh from the Muslims will not be sent back to the Muslims.

It initially looked unfavourable for the Muslims, with some of the Muslims feeling that all of the Quraysh's demands were being met.

However, it enabled the Muslims to concentrate on building their community in Medina, without fear of attack. It also indirectly recognised the Islamic state of Medina.

The Treaty was signed under the tree at Hudaibiyyah and was written by 'Ali ibn Abi Talib ر. At one point it was demanded by the Quraysh that 'Ali cross out the phrase 'Messenger of Allah' under the name of Muhammad ﷺ. The Quraysh said that this was disputed because if they believed that then there would be no problem. 'Ali ر could not do this as it felt so wrong to him, so the Prophet ﷺ asked where this was written and he himself crossed out the phrase.

The Treaty of Hudaibiyyah was broken by one of the Quraysh allied tribes. This meant the Muslims had a right to go to Makkah and perform 'Umrah or Hajj. They knew they would not be welcomed, so the Prophet Muhammad ﷺ decided to go with the entire army and peacefully reunite the Muslims with the beloved Holy City. On the 10th Ramadan, 10,000 Muslim soldiers set off with the Prophet ﷺ, with another 2,000 joining them along on the way. When they arrived outside Makkah, the Prophet ﷺ instructed every man to light a fire so that the Quraysh would over-estimate the size of the army.

When they arrived on the 18th of Ramadan, the Prophet ﷺ divided the army to enter at the same time from the four different entrances to Makkah and ordered them to go peacefully and avoid fighting.

The only skirmish that took place was in the North-East when Ikramah ر and Sufwan ر attacked Khalid's ر troops with swords and bows. After a short fight, the Muslims won, losing only two men and the Quraysh, twelve.

Abu Sufyan ر, the chief of the Quraysh, then accepted Islam.

"Say, the Truth has come and falsehood gone.
Verily falsehood is bound to vanish." (al-Isra 17:81)

The Prophet ﷺ then said, *"He who enters the house of Abu Sufyan will be safe, He who lays down arms will be safe, He who locks his door will be safe."*

The Prophet Muhammad ﷺ, then entered the Ka'aba with 'Ali ibn Abu Talib ﺝ and removed all the idols that had been there.

Bilal ﺝ then climbed to the top of the Ka'aba and called out the Adhan. The people then gathered around the Ka'aba, and the Prophet ﷺ said to everyone gathered:

"There is no God but Allah. He has no associates. He has made good his promise that He held to His bondman and helped him and defeated all the confederates. Bear in mind that every claim of privilege, whether that of blood or property is abolished except that of the custody of the Ka'aba and of supplying water to the pilgrims. Bear in mind that for anyone who is slain the blood money is one hundred camels. People of

Quraysh, surely God has abolished all pride from you from the time of ignorance and all pride in your ancestry, because all men are descended from Adam, and Adam was made of clay." (Muslim)

He then turned to the people and asked, "O Quraysh, what treatment do you expect of me?"

They said, "Mercy, O Prophet of Allah. We expect nothing but good from you."

The Prophet ﷺ replied, "Today I will speak to you as Yusuf spoke to his brothers. I will not harm you and Allah will forgive you, for He is Merciful and Loving. Go, you are free."

The Prophet ﷺ recited this *Ayat* from the Qur'an:

"No reproach this day shall be on you; Allah will forgive you; He is the Most Merciful of the Merciful." (Yusuf 12:92)

THE MERCY OF THE PROPHET ﷺ

Even though the Makkans had been unspeakably cruel, waged war on the Muslims, killed his uncle Hamza ﺝ in a horrendous way, still the Prophet ﷺ did not seek revenge, even though this would have been easy. Instead, he allowed everyone to go free. At this point, the whole of Makkah embraced Islam.

The Prophet ﷺ forgave the slave who killed his uncle, and Hind ﺝ, who had ordered the killing and eaten his uncle's liver. When they became Muslim, they wanted to see the Prophet ﷺ but even though the Prophet ﷺ was glad they embraced Islam, he did not wish to see them as it reminded him of that difficult day.

After the conquest of Makkah, emissaries came from all over Arabia, and within a short space of time, the whole of Arabia was united under the banner of Islam.

"God has made Makkah a sanctuary since the day He created the Heavens and the Earth, and it will remain a sanctuary by virtue of the sanctity God has bestowed on it until the Day of Resurrection. It (fighting in it) was not made lawful to anyone before me. Nor will it be made lawful to anyone after me, and it was not made lawful for me except for a short period of time." (al-Bukhari)

*See note on page 62

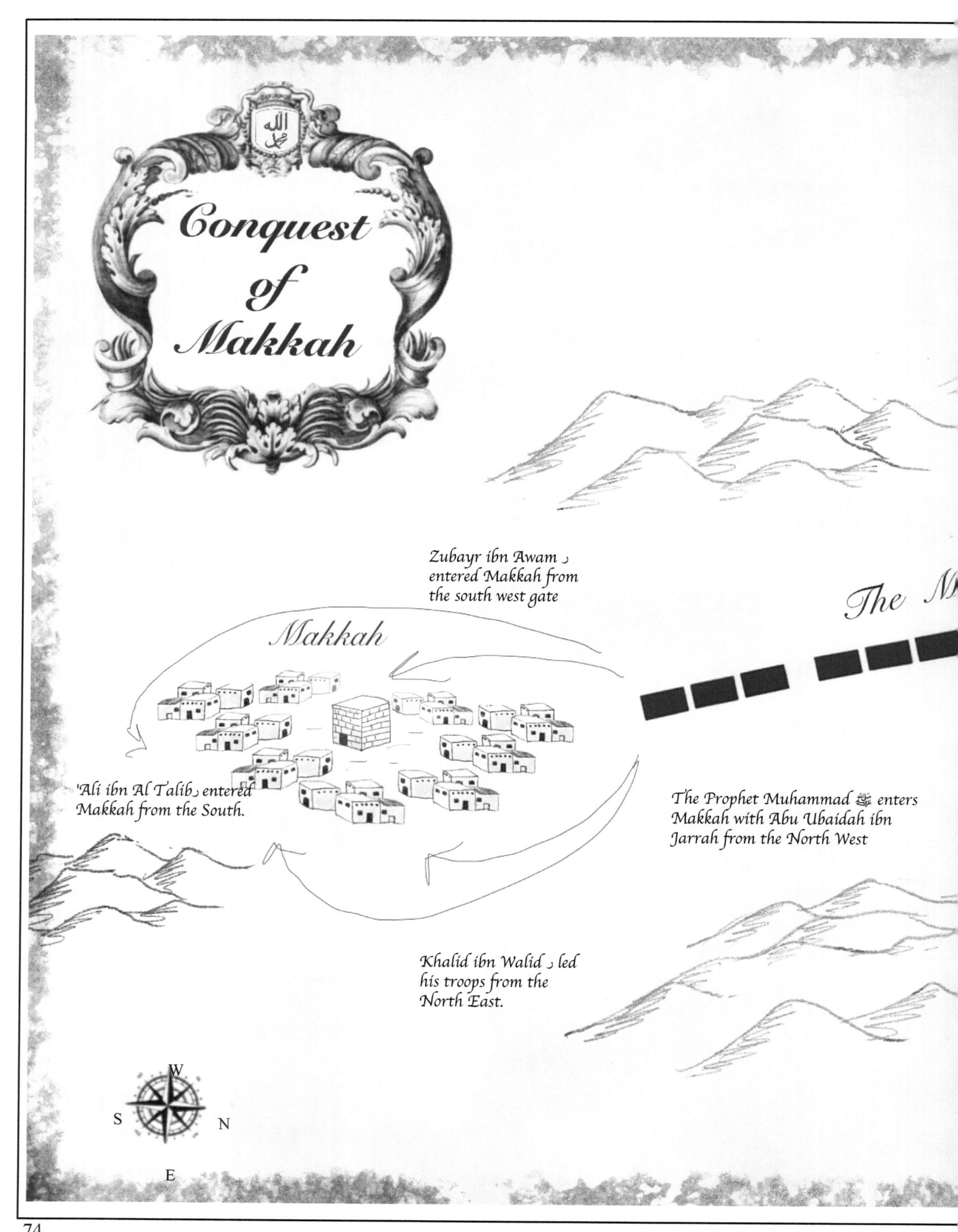

Conquest of Makkah

Zubayr ibn Awam ﵁ entered Makkah from the south west gate

Makkah

The N...

'Ali ibn Al Talib ﵁ entered Makkah from the South.

The Prophet Muhammad ﷺ enters Makkah with Abu Ubaidah ibn Jarrah from the North West

Khalid ibn Walid ﵁ led his troops from the North East.

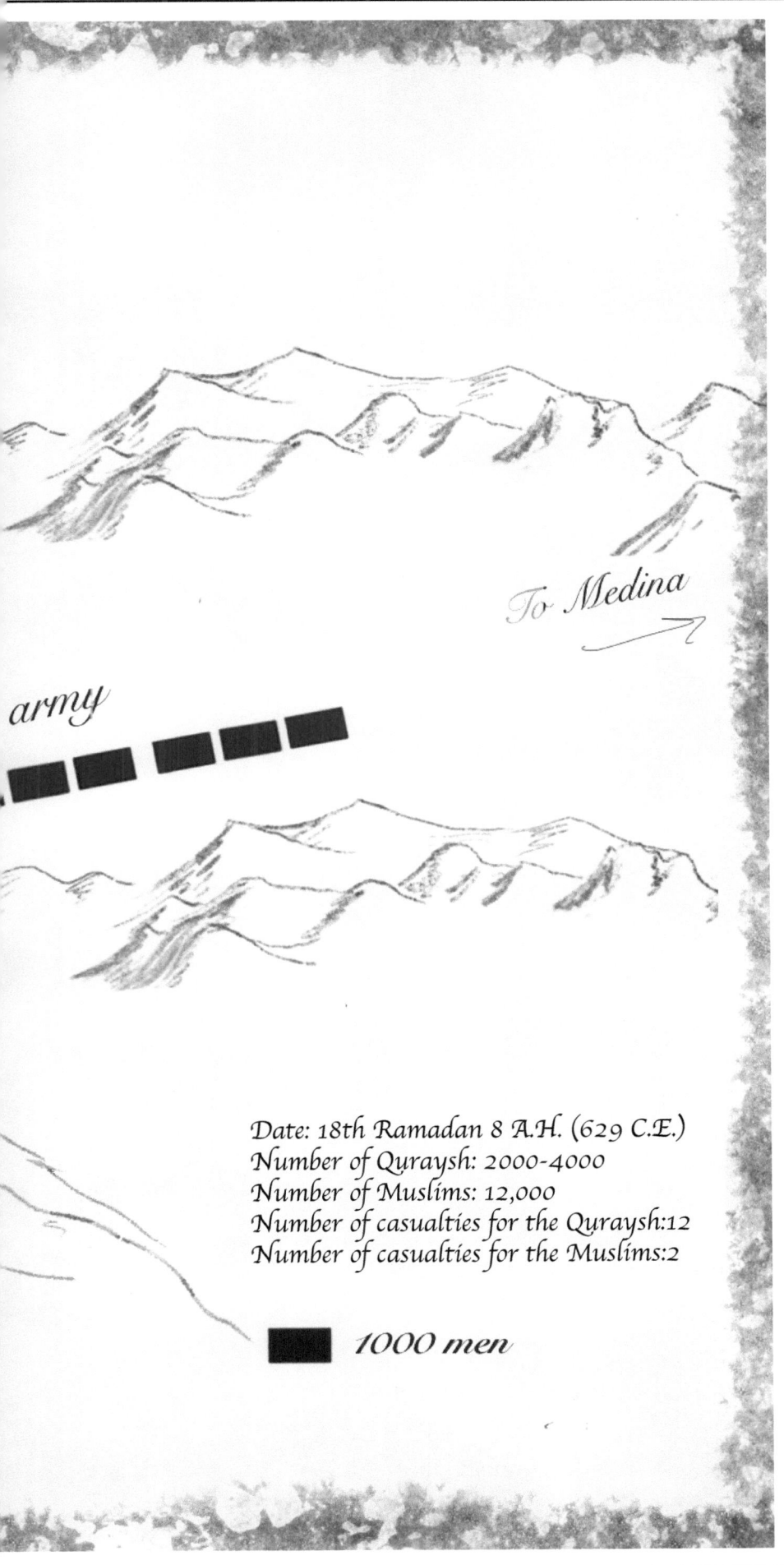

To Medina

army

Date: 18th Ramadan 8 A.H. (629 C.E.)
Number of Quraysh: 2000-4000
Number of Muslims: 12,000
Number of casualties for the Quraysh:12
Number of casualties for the Muslims:2

1000 men

"O Mankind! We created you from a single pair of male and female, and made you into nations and tribes only so that you may recognise and identify each other. Verily of you the most honoured in Allah's reckoning is the one who is the most righteous and God-fearing among you. Certainly Allah is full of all knowledge and knows best in all things."

(Al Hujurat 49:13)

The Prophet ﷺ said, "God has made Makkah a sanctuary since the day He created the Heavens and the Earth, and it will remain a sanctuary by virtue of the sanctity God has bestowed on it until the Day of Resurrection. It (fighting in it) was not made lawful to anyone before me. Nor will it be made lawful to anyone after me, and it was not made lawful for me except for a short period of time." (al-Bukhari)

Battle of Hunayn

After the conquest of Makkah, there only remained the area of Ta'if, where the tribes of Banu Saqeef and Banu Hawazin lived. They were a proud people and considered themselves almost as important as the Quraysh. They now felt it was their duty to stand up and repel the new religion. Until this point, they had not assisted the Quraysh in their battles with the Prophet Muhammad ﷺ. Ta'if was the place where the Prophet ﷺ had been badly tormented by them, having rocks hurled at him after he tried to preach about Islam eight years before.

They remembered their aggression and assumed the Prophet ﷺ would come to take revenge. The two tribes were skilled warriors and archers. They felt it best to go on the offence and attack first. All of their smaller linked tribes then joined the attack. They brought their women and children as well and headed toward Makkah where the Prophet ﷺ was still positioned.

It would have been strategically more advantageous to stay inside Makkah but the Prophet ﷺ, who wanted to avoid bloodshed and wanted to keep battle away from the sacred area of the Ka'aba, decided to go and meet the enemy outside Makkah.

To equip the army, the Prophet ﷺ took a loan from some wealthy Makkans and a loan of armour from others. He could have just taken these things, as he had just conquered Makkah, but this was not the way of the Prophet ﷺ, who conducted himself with honour and nobility at all times.

The Prophet ﷺ leaving Makkah behind him, with all his army, could have been an ideal opportunity for the Makkans to reclaim their capital but this did not happen, as they had all embraced Islam.

The Muslim army of 12,000 was, for a change, greater than the enemies' army, of only 4,000. This, along with good armour and supplies produced over-confidence among the Muslims who now felt themselves unbeatable.

As they arrived, they found that the tribes of Ta'if had a better position strategically. This did not deter the Muslims, who, in their confidence, did not even order themselves into formations when they started the battle.

Arrows rained down on the Muslims and they backed up in disarray. The initial onslaught was heavy, although very few were killed, it had the effect of unnerving the Muslims.

The Prophet ﷺ, undeterred, began steadily marching towards the enemy, declaring, *"I am the Prophet, which is nothing but the*

truth; I am the offspring of 'Abdul-Muttalib."

This had a calming and soothing effect on the men, who regrouped and strengthened their resolve.

As the Muslims had earlier faltered, the Ta'ifians came out onto the battlefield so now the Muslims could engage them in hand to hand fighting. The enemy was repelled and the situation completely reversed. In no time at all the Ta'ifians surrendered.

The opponents ran in disarray but were not able to travel quickly with the women and children. Many men, women and children were captured, as well as a many animals and weapons.

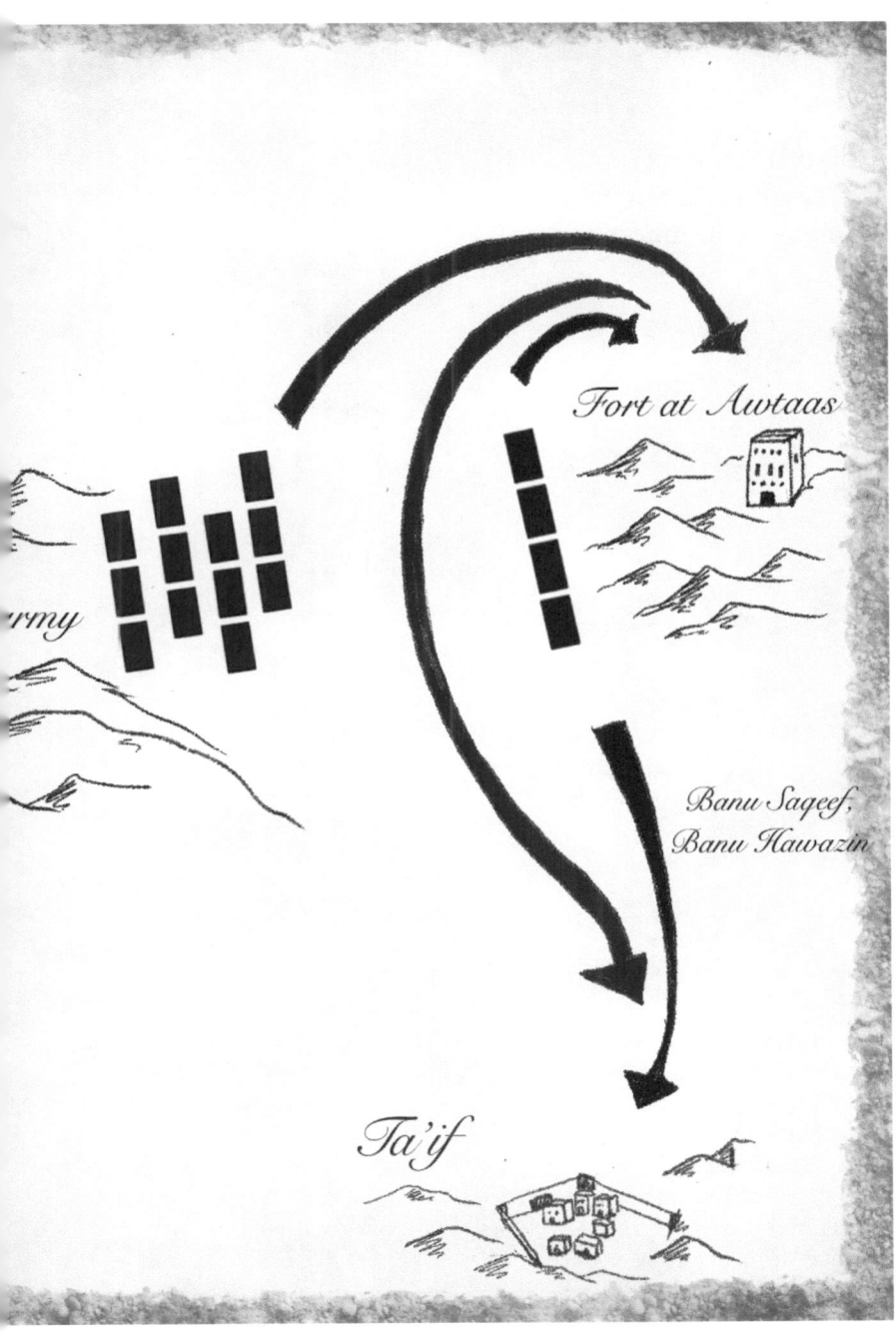

Fort at Awtaas

Banu Saqeef, Banu Hawazin

Ta'if

rmy

The retreating army then scattered; some went to the Awtaas fort, and the others went to Ta'if, which had fortified walls surrounding it.

Awtaas was easily defeated, with more captives being taken, the Muslim army then headed towards Ta'if and laid siege. Ta'if had plenty of provisions and the walls were strong. The Muslims for the first time used catapults, but they proved ineffective against the fireballs that were hurled at them from the walls.

The siege lasted 20 days. The Prophet ﷺ did not want to be away from Medina for so long and decided to abandon the siege. He also felt confident that it would not be too long until they declared their faith in Islam. Some asked him ﷺ to curse the tribes at Ta'if, but the Prophet refused and prayed for them to be guided.

After the battle, the captives numbered about 6,000, many of whom had been distributed to the Muslims, then the tribe leader of the Hawazin came to request the release of the prisoners. The Prophet ﷺ, according to his nature, suggested to the Muslims to release the prisoners for free, but those who wanted to could claim compensation. Most released them for free, although some who were poor asked for the compensation, which was given out of the Muslims' own treasury.

The Banu Hawazin were impressed by this generosity and many became Muslim.

About six months later, the chief of Ta'if, presented himself at Medina and became Muslim along with many other remaining outlying tribes.

After this, the whole of Arabia came under the banner of Islam.

"And when came the help of Allah and triumph, and you witnessed the people entering Islam crowd upon crowd."
(An-Nasr 110: 1-2)

The Byzantines

The Byzantine Empire, the extension of the Christian Roman Empire, spanned from year 330-1453 and covered large areas of Asia, Southern Europe and Northern Africa and was the largest empire in the time of the Prophet ﷺ.

Raphael's student's painting of Constantine I's vision of the Cross, 16th century.

The Byzantine Empire was the eastern side of the huge Roman Empire which began in Rome in 27 B.C. and stretched as far as Scotland in the U.K. and to Carthage in North Africa. The Roman Empire began to decline around 212 A.D. during the reign of the corrupt Emperor Commodus who saw himself god-like. Emperor Commodus is featured in the film, 'Gladiator'. The great Roman Empire then changed *"...from a kingdom of gold to one of rust and iron."* (Greek historian, Dio Cassius) The Empire split into two, the Western Roman Empire and the Eastern Roman Empire, or the Byzantine Empire. The Western Roman Empire began to break apart with invasions from Germanic tribes and ended in 476. The Byzantine Empire continued until the fall of Constantinople in 1453.

Flavius Heraclius (575-641) was the Emperor of the Byzantine Empire from 610 to 641.

Heraclius drove the Persians out of Asia Minor, defeating them decisively in 627 at the battle of Nineveh. The Persian King, Khosrow II was overthrown and executed by his son Kavad II, who wanted peaceful relations with the Byzantines.

Heraclius married twice, first to Fabia Eudokia and then to his niece Martina, which was strongly looked down upon by the church. He had two children with Fabia (Eudoxia Epiphania and Emperor Constantine III) and at least nine children with Martina, but they were very sickly.

Heraclius was long remembered favourably by the Western Church for his reputed recovery of the True Cross from the Persians. After a tour of the Empire, Heraclius returned the cross to Jerusalem.

The 14th century Muslim scholar, Ibn Kathir (d. 1371) writes that; "Heraclius was one of the wisest and amongst the most resolute, shrewd, and opinionated of kings. He ruled the Romans with great leadership and splendour."

He also received the letter from the Prophet Muhammad ﷺ, inviting him to Islam as we saw on page 21.

Battle of Mu'tah

Battle duration: Few days
Byzantine army: 100,000+
Muslim army: 3,000

Byzantine casualties: Unknown
Muslim casualties: 12+

The Battle of Mu'tah took place in 629 (8 A.H.) in north of Arabia, near the Byzantine borders, where they were reoccupying territory from the Persians.

The Muslims were having trouble in that region from the Byzantines, who would raid their caravans and intimidate the Muslims. This escalated to the killing of an envoy, al-Harith ibn 'Umayr al-'Azdi ﻬ that the Prophet ﷺ had sent to the king of Busraa, Shurahbeel ibn 'Amr Al-Ghassaani.

The Prophet ﷺ then assembled an army of about 3,000 men. He said to the commanders:

"Go forth in the Name of Allah, in the cause of Allah and fight those who disbelieve in Allah. Proceed, but neither break pledges, act unfaithfully in regard to the booty, mutilate the killed, commit infanticide, nor kill the recluses in their monasteries." (Ahmad)

"If Zayd ibn Harithah ﻬ is wounded, let Ja'far ibn Abu Talib ﻬ succeed him. If Ja'far is wounded, let 'Abdullah ibn Rawaahah ﻬ succeed him." (al-Bukhari and Muslim)

The Muslim army arrived and found out that the Byzantine number could be as many as 100,000 men. They sought counsel with each other, unsure of what to do. Perhaps they should turn back, or should they stay and fight? Then Zayd ﻬ said:

"O people, what you hate is the thing for which you set out — martyrdom. We do not fight others by virtue of troops, military gear or multitudes. We fight them by virtue of this religion with which Allah the Almighty honoured us. Proceed and it will be one of two things, either gaining victory or martyrdom."

The soldiers agreed with these truthful words and prepared to fight.

The two armies then engaged and fought relentlessly. Zayd ibn Harithah ﻬ was the first leader from the Muslims to be martyred whilst he was fighting courageously. Therefore, Ja'far ibn 'abu Talib ﻬ took the standard with his right hand and chanted lines of poetry referring to Paradise and his determination to fight the Romans.

His right arm was cut off, so he held the standard with his left hand, which was also cut off. He therefore enfolded the standard using the upper parts of his arms until he was martyred. 'Abdullah ibn Rawahah ﻬ grabbed the standard and endeavored to dismount from his horse.

Divine revelation informed the Prophet ﷺ about what was happening a thousand miles away. Anas narrated that the Prophet ﷺ announced that Zayd, Ja'far and Ibn Rawahah, may Allah be pleased with them, were martyred. It is reported that the Prophet ﷺ said: *"Zayd took the standard until he was martyred. Then Ja'far took it until he was martyred. Then Ibn Rawahah took it until he was martyred."* The Prophet ﷺ then shed plentiful tears and said: *"Then a sword from the swords of Allah took it until Allah the Almighty granted them victory." (Al-Bukhari)*

Khalid ibn al-Walid ﻬ was the sword that the Prophet ﷺ was referring to. He was given the standard and assumed control of the army. He thought about what to do. He wanted to give the impression that new reinforcements had come to aid the Muslims. That day, they kept their ground on the battlefield until night. He then repositioned the troops and made a huge noise with the cavalry and clouds of dust. This worked, as the Byzantines thought reinforcements had arrived. Khalid then launched a fierce attack the next morning. It is reported he broke nine swords with nothing remaining except a Yemeni sabre.

The Byzantines retreated. Historians are unsure why. Perhaps believing the Muslims numbered too many, or maybe tired of the battle and needing provisions.

The Muslims then returned home, back to Medina - much to the joy of those waiting for them. It was not a decisive victory, but it was a huge achievement all the same, to ward off the attack of an experienced Byzantine army.

Expedition of Tabuk

The three thousand Muslim strong army crossed the deserts of Arabia to Tabuk, almost 700 miles away.

As the Muslims became stronger and their numbers grew, the Jews, some of the Arab Christians of the North of Arabia, and the hypocrites amongst the Muslims, grew worried. The only way they could think of to remove this new religion was to ask the most powerful Emperor of the time, the Byzantine Emperor, Flavius Heraclius.

They sent envoys to persuade Heraclius to invade Arabia, telling him, falsely, that Arabia was in disarray, that the Quraysh had been conquered and Arabia was now open to anyone to march in and take over. Emperor Heraclius was tempted, especially when he remembered the humiliating defeat of his army of 100,000 men, by a small army of only 3,000 Muslims, a year before at the Battle of Mu'tah. He wanted to remove the blot in his military history and add the Arabian Peninsula to his empire.

Heraclius ordered all the surrounding areas to prepare for battle by sending in troops. They were to gather at Balqa, a town on the north-eastern borders of Arabia. The army was set to be about 300,000 men.

The Prophet ﷺ received intelligence about this and considered what to do. At the time, it was a hot summer, with date crops failing, but the Prophet ﷺ, knew that decisive action needed to be taken before Heraclius had time to gather his armies. The tactic of digging a trench and defending themselves in Medina would not have worked against such a great and trained army, who were well used to these tactics.

The Prophet ﷺ decided to march to the frontiers. He asked for donations to equip and prepare the army. Abu Bakr ﵁ donated all of his wealth and Sayyidina 'Umar ﵁ donated half. The hypocrites, on the other hand, were quite worried about this development, as they had not expected the Prophet ﷺ to make such a bold move, and now they would have to join the battle. They decided to create doubt in some of the Muslims, about the harsh heat of the desert, the huge and powerful armies of the Byzantine Empire and other disheartening speeches. The Qur'an mentions them:

"Even if they had come out with you they would have not added to your strength but would have only done mischief through efforts at creating discord among your ranks..." (At-Tawbah 9:47-48)

There was not a shortage of numbers of men who wished to join the Prophet ﷺ, in fact, there were so many that there were not enough camels for them to ride on and so some were not able to join, much to their great sadness.

In all, the Muslim army numbered 30,000. They prepared for the long march in the intense heat in the month of Rajab 630. The army, although used to desert conditions, became so thirsty that they were forced to kill some of the camels to obtain the water stored in their humps.

The Muslim army arrived at Tabuk, a strategic place to view the borders. They indeed had been correct in their decisive and quick march as the Emperor was still in Constantinople gathering troops

"Nor any blame on those who came to you with a request to provide them with mounts and you said to them: I am unable to provide mounts for you." And they returned with tears flowing from their eyes out of grief that they had no means of their own to spend." (At-Tawbah 9:92)

Solidus of Justinian II, second reign, after 705

and provisions and the Christian Arabs were not ready to mobilise. When they saw the Muslim army arrive, they became unnerved as the move was so courageous and unexpected that they stayed in their towns, unwilling to fight.

The Emperor, hearing that the Prophet ﷺ and his army had arrived at the borders, lost his enthusiasm, feeling caught out and unprepared, so he cancelled the invasion. Instead, he fortified his position, in case the Prophet ﷺ decided to attack. However, this was never the Prophet's ﷺ intention. His intention was to protect Medina and Arabia against the Byzantine invasion.

The Muslim army stayed in the region of Tabuk for a short time, talking with the border tribes, who being very impressed with the Prophet's ﷺ leadership, agreed to come under the protection of the Muslims. They also agreed to pay the *jizya*, the tax for non-Muslims under Muslim rule.

Now the Muslim lands stretched as far as the very northernmost borders of Arabia, which not only was the beginning of the Byzantine Empire but also the great Persian Empire.

The Muslims then returned home, much to the great joy of those they left behind. Medina now felt secure against attack and the Prophet ﷺ again arrived in their midst.

WHAT IS JIZYA?

Like zakat, which is the tax of 2.5% of extra wealth which most Muslims have to pay, the *jizya* is specifically for non-Muslims. The amount would vary in different Khalifates, but started at one dirham per year (4.234 grams of gold). The amount also varied according to income. Sayyidina 'Umar ﺭ set the rate at four dirhams for the wealthy, two for the middle class and one for the working class. The money would then go to the Bayt al-Mal, the government treasury for social care, administration and other government expenses. For reference, one dinar was approximately equivalent to two to three days of family expenditure. In return, the Muslim state would protect and care for its members, including negotiating the release of any of them from capture. The non-Muslims are to receive the same advantages as the Muslims. It is also stated that it needs to be collected with leniency and politeness.

Not everyone had to pay it. Those exempt were: women, children, the elderly, disabled, the ill, both physically and mentally, monks, hermits and slaves. Also, those who could not afford to pay.

The Prophet Muhammad's ﷺ Farewell Speech

Plain of Arafat, 9th Dhul Hijjah 10 AH

After the conquest of Makkah, the Muslims were able to perform Hajj. It is reported that 100,000 Muslims joined him on Hajj that year. These are some highlights of the sermon he ﷺ made on the plain of 'Arafat, just three months before his passing to the next life.

"O People, lend me an attentive ear, for I know not whether after this year I shall ever be among you again. Therefore, listen carefully to what I am saying and take these words to those who could not be present here today."

"Regard the life and property of every Muslim as a sacred trust. Hurt no one so that no one may hurt you. Remember that you will indeed meet your Lord, and that He will indeed reckon your actions."

"O People! No prophet or apostle will come after me and no new faith will be born...I leave behind you two things, the Qur'an and the Sunnah and if you follow these, you will never go astray."

"O People, listen to me carefully, worship Allah, say your five daily prayers, fast during the month of Ramadan, and give your wealth in *zakat*. Perform Hajj if you can afford it."

"Beware of Shaytan, for the safety of your religion. He has lost all hope that he will be able to lead you astray in big things, so beware of following him in small things."

"All mankind is from Adam and Eve, an Arab has no superiority over a non-Arab nor a non-Arab have superiority over an Arab; also a white has no superiority over a black nor a black has any superiority over a white except by piety and good action."

"O People, it is true that you have certain rights with regard to your women but they also have rights over you. Remember that you have taken them as wives, only with Allah's trust and permission. If they abide by your right then to them belongs the right to be fed and clothed in kindness. Do treat your women well and be kind to them for they are your partners and committed helpers... "

Towards the end of the sermon, the Prophet ﷺ asked, "O people, have I faithfully delivered to you my message?" A powerful murmur rose in agreement which rolled like thunder throughout the valley from thousands of pilgrims. "O Allah, Yes!" they all said together. Prophet ﷺ raised his forefinger and said, "O Allah, bear witness that I have conveyed your message to your people."

The Passing of the Prophet ﷺ to the Next Life

The Prophet ﷺ fell ill on the 28th or 29th of Safar, 11 A.H., and some days later took to his bed, with fever and headache, in his wife 'Aisha's ؓ house who read countless prayers for him. With great effort he continued to lead the prayers until his illness became so great he could not stand. He requested for Abu Bakr ؓ to lead the prayers in his stead.

He said that Allah offered him ﷺ a choice to stay in this world or to be with his Friend in Heaven. The Prophet ﷺ chose to be with Allah ﷻ.

The Prophet Muhammad ﷺ died with his head in the lap of 'Aisha ؓ.

After he passed, there was great confusion among the Muslims. Many could not believe he had really died, including 'Umar ؓ who said he would the cut the head off anyone who said the Prophet ﷺ was dead. Then Hadrat Abu Bakr ؓ recited this verse, after which 'Umar ؓ calmed and said that it was like he had heard the verse for the first time:

"Muhammad is no more than a messenger: many were the Messengers that passed away before Him. If he died or was slain, will ye then turn back on your heels? If any did turn back on his heels, not the least harm will he do to Allah; but Allah (on the other hand) will swiftly reward those who (serve him) with gratitude." (Aali Imran 3:144)

Hadrat 'Ali ؓ washed the body of the Prophet ﷺ and he was buried in 'Aisha's room. His Companions then visited him, one after the other, including the ladies.

'Anas ؓ said: "I have never witnessed a day better or brighter than that day on which the Messenger of Allah ﷺ came to us; and I have never witnessed a more awful or darker day than that one on which the Messenger of Allah ﷺ died."

Masjid an-Nawabi or the Prophet's Mosque where the Prophet Muhammad ﷺ is buried in Medina, Saudi Arabia

Timeline of the Life of Prophet Muhammad ﷺ

571

Birth of the Prophet Muhammad ﷺ. Muhammad's ﷺ father dies before he is born. Also known as the Year of the Elephant.

577

Muhammad ﷺ is returned to mother Amina ر but she dies soon after. He goes to live with his uncle 'Abdul Mutallib.

579

'Abdul Muttalib dies. Muhammad ﷺ goes to live with his grandfather Abu Talib.

583

First visit to Syria with trading caravan.

616

Hadrat Hamza ر and Hadrat 'Umar ر accept Islam.

615

His son, Hadrat Qasim ر dies.

A group of Muslims migrate to Abyssina.

614

Muhammad ﷺ begins to openly preach with much opposition from the Quraysh, and the Muslims were expelled from Makkah.

610

First revelation from the Angel Jibrael.

619

The Year of Sadness

Hadrat Abu Talib and Sayyidatina Khadija ر pass away.

Visit to Ta'if.

620

Marriage to Hadrat Sau'da ر, an older widow and Hadrat 'Aisha ر, the youngest of his wives and later to be a great scholar.

621

First pledge of Aq'ba

622 (1A.H.)

The migration to Medina (The Hijra).

632 (10 A.H.)

The Farewell Pilgrimage with Hajj being obligatory. The Prophet Muhammad ﷺ passes to the next life on 12th Rabi al-Awwal.

630 (8 A.H.)

Marriage with Hadrat Maimuna ر.

Birth of son, Ibrahim ر.

629 (7 A.H.)

The Conquest of Mecca. Tribes come from far and wide to embrace Islam.

Battle of Ta'if and Hunayn

Battle of Tabuk

629 (7 A.H.)

Battle of Khaybar

Marriage with Hadrat Safiyya ر.

First 'Umra performed.

586

Muhammad ﷺ, aged 15, was part of a treaty dedicated to upholding justice in central Arabia.

595

Second trade expedition for Sayyidanita Khadija ر, whom Muhammad ﷺ marries that year.

598

Birth of son Hadrat Qasim ر.

600

Birth of daughter, Hadrat Zainab ر.

603

Birth of daughter Hadrat Ruqayya ر.

607

Birth of son 'Abdullah ibn Muhammad ر.

605

Birth of daughter Hadrat Zainab ر.

Also the rennovation of the Ka'aba

604

Birth of daughter Umm Kulthum ر.

624 (3 A.H.)

The place of prayer is directed towards Makkah.

Fasting the month of Ramadan becomes obligatory.

Paying zakat becomes obligatory.

624 (3 A.H.)

Battle of Badr

625 (4 A.H.)

Marriage with Hadrat Hafsa ر, a pious widow and Hadrat Zainab ر, a divorcee, later that year.

625 (4 A.H.)

Battle of Uhud

628 (7 A.H.)

Treaty of Hudaibiyya.

Marriage with Hadrat Habiba ر, a divorcee.

627 (6 A.H.)

Battle of the Trench

627 (6 A.H.)

Marriage with Hadrat Zaynab bint Hajash ر. The revelation for the rule of modesty.

626 (5 A.H.)

Marriage to Hadrat Umm Salama ر, a widow with many children and Hadrat Jawariya ر, daughter of a tribal cheiftan.

Jihad in Modern Times: Jihad of the Hand

HOW CAN WE MAKE THIS WORLD A BETTER PLACE?

The Prophet Muhammad ﷺ encouraged excellence in all things, whether a simple task or leading nations. He liked people to help others and to be positive members of the community. There are many ways in our modern world to make a society better, from a street cleaner to a president.

We use our hands to do things, to fix things, to make things. Jihad of the hand includes almost everything that we can think of that makes society a better place including building, transport, communication, social care and medicine.

Some of the many examples of jobs that help build a better and safer community include social workers, engineers, city planners, teachers, doctors, nurses, police, aid workers and helping the homeless.

Some of the most essential jobs often go unnoticed; what about the dustbin workers, waking early every morning?

Muslim Hands is a charity supporting some of the most vulnerable societies around the world.

MUSLIM CHARITIES

Muslims, along with Christians give the most charity, according to a U.K. poll in 2012 with over 70% of Muslims giving charity every year. According to this poll, Muslims gave an average of £432/year, Christians £580, Jewish people £316, then atheists £133/year.

There are many global Muslim charities that work tirelessly around the world for disaster relief, building wells, helping orphans, refugees, those in poverty, and other humanitarian aid.

Small charities are also essential for local communities such as women's refuges, youth offending programmes, food banks and more.

SOCIAL ENTERPRISE

A social enterprise is a business that makes money to operate, but benefits the community. This can involve employing people in the third world to give them financial independence or benefits people directly by providing services to support them.

A farmer in Indonesia

One social enterprise called iGrow, helps underemployed farmers to grow by connecting landowners, farmers and investors so that crops are grown and then sold, making money for all the farmers as well as the investors.

Another social enterprise, the Casserole Club, connects cooks at home with elderly people in their area to relieve loneliness and to provide healthy home cooked meals.

Have you got an ingenious idea to solve environmental problems, food poverty, homelessness or support those with their mental health?

Think about some of the problems that your community or country faces - how could these problems be solved?

Starting small and creating a model that works is the key to success. If it is a good idea, a team will form around you and you can work together to make wonderful things happen.

Takula makes bags and accessories from locally sourced fabrics, supporting the local community.

SCIENCE

Islam embraces the sciences with the Muslim world historically pioneering many new discoveries to help make the world a better place.

Professor Abdus Salam won the Nobel prize in 1979 for his work in particle physics when he laid the groundwork for the discovery of the Higgs Boson particle - one that is responsible for giving all other particles mass.

He was born to a poor family in Pakistan and was given preferential treatment so that he could do his studies after his father had a dream about him. He recited the Qur'an when he received his Nobel Prize.

Dr. Ahmed Zewail is an Egyptian born physicist and one of the best-known scientists in recent history. He was a professor at the University of California and developed ultrafast lasers and ways to propel electrons to study their behaviours. He won the Nobel prize in 1999 due to his discovery of the femtosecond - the smallest part of the second to be measured.

Dr. Hayat Sindi has made major contributions to biochemistry and is a visiting scholar to Harvard. She has won many awards including the Al Mukaramah prize for scientific innovation by Prince Khalid bin Faisel al-Saud. She has also become a UNESCO ambassador, encouraging Muslim women across the Arab world. She also developed stamp-sized lab tests for poorer countries to give immediate test results.

Jihad of Education and Counsel

Writing books, opening schools and Universities and teaching the population about Islam are all forms of Jihad.

The Muslim world saw the largest libraries and centres for education in the world open up almost one thousand years ago. Islamic scholars spend their lives studying the religion, sometimes writing books and teaching others. With todays social media, knowledge can be accessed by more and more people around the world.

Sheikh Hisham Kabbani, a respected scholar and descendant of the Prophet Muhammad ﷺ, defines Jihad in his book of the same title as:

"Removing all misconceptions and stereotypes in clarifying the image of Islam held by non-Muslims, building a trusting relationship and working with them in ways that accord with their way of thinking, are all primary forms of Jihad. Similarly, establishing a strong community and nation which can fulfill all physical needs of its people, thereby creating for them conditions in which the message will be heard, rather than being lost in the strife and struggle of everyday life, are requirements and form a basic building block of the Jihadic concept. These foundations fulfill the Qur'anic injunction, *"Let there arise out of you a band of people inviting to all that is good, enjoining what is right, and forbidding what is wrong: and these it is that shall be successful."* (Al-Imran 3:104) Until this is accomplished the conditions of Jihad remain unfulfilled."

Speaking out against oppression and injustice is an essential part. When ISIS took control of Syria, Islamic scholars from around the world condemned their actions including Sheikh Muhammad al-Yaqoubi who had to escape Syria when attempts were made to silence him. In an interview with CNN, he condemned ISIL and said, "We have to speak loud and very clear that Muslims and Islam have nothing to do with this... ISIS has no nationality. Its nationality is terror, savagery, and hatred."

Scholars are experts in the Shar'iah, the Islamic law. It is the duty of

Sheikh Muhammad al-Yaqoubi, descended from a long line of Islamic scholars.

Al-Azhar University in Cairo was founded in 970 or 972 during the Fatimid Khalifate and is the oldest degree granting University in the world and is also the most prestigious University for Islamic learning. It oversees a worldwide network of over 2 million students.

every Muslim to learn and familiarise themselves with the Shar'iah. This is to help their journey in Islam, both on a personal level and a community level and also to prevent ignorance which is the main cause of problems such as extremism and fanaticism.

Scholars can also make fatwas or legal rulings about many issues including the prohibition of domestic violence and other important matters.

DA'WAH AND INTERFAITH

Da'wah, or 'inviting to Islam' is a central part of the religion. To help non-Muslims understand more about the faith and, if God Wills it, to be blessed with accepting Islam.

Islam is unique in all the world religions in being able to stand up to logical cross-examination.

Logic is studied in Islam to develop our mind's capacity to use reason. Scholars may use reason, for example, to develop legal rulings and to explain and discuss relgious ideas with others.

Sayyidina 'Ali, the Prophet's ﷺ son-in-law, was an example of eloquence, intelligence and reason. Non-Muslims in his day would come and hear his lectures and debate the various points in the religion, many of whom became Muslim.

There are many interfaith programmes that help to bridge the gap between religions.

Respect and tolerance for other religions is very important in Islam as indicated in the Qur'an and exemplified by the Prophet Muhammad ﷺ.

Jihad of the Sword

Are there any valid reasons for Jihad of the sword in this day and age? This is a hugely important question that concerns all Muslims and young people of today.

This question has been clearly answered by many scholars such as Sheikh Hisham Kabbani and Sheikh Muhammad Yaqoubi, based on scholarly evidence by the examination of the Sunnah and the Qur'an.

MODERN LEGAL RULING ON COMBATIVE JIHAD

What is combative Jihad? It is, according to Sheikh Hisham's fatwa, 'the declaration of war against belligerent aggressors.'

This means an aggressive group of people or a nation who stubbornly want to fight, ignoring diplomatic solutions, and ignoring reason and peaceful solutions. Also having the intention to wipe out another group by killing or enslaving.

In this case, the leader of the Muslim community can opt for Jihad of the Sword to defend the faith and protect the people.

It is important to remember that combative Jihad is only used when "...combat is forced on you by the invasion of your country." (Sheikh Yusuf al-Qaradawi) and is not when a break-away faction declares Jihad as we see in extremist militant groups.

Sheikh Muhammad Hisham Kabbani, an emminent scholar from the Middle East and the United States issued a fatwa about Jihad in modern times.

From Sheikh Hisham Kabbani's fatwa: When is it permissible to fight?:

- When diplomatic solutions have failed.
- When an aggressive group of people or nation is intent on fighting and has declared war.
- When Muslims have been expelled from a land, from their legally owned houses and jobs.
- When the appointed ruler of the country has considered all options, tried all diplomatic means, and then decided to do so.

The ruler of the Muslims may then declare combative Jihad. People in the country cannot decide to take up arms without the permission of the ruler.

And in these modern days, there is no Muslim country that honours all of the Islamic predicates and therefore there is no recognised khalif to lead the Muslims. Without a khalif, there can be no declaration of Jihad (of the sword).

Sheikh Hisham states: "There is no Jihad in the Islamic lands. While undoubtedly there is combat taking place, there is no Jihad taking place."

(Sheikh Hisham's fatwa can be read in full in his book entitled, Jihad, Principles of Leadership in War and Peace, 2010.)

Many Muslims are members of the armed forces in the West.

ARMAGEDDON

We may be nearing the times that the Holy Prophet ﷺ was talking in this hadith:
Abu Hurayrah (may Allah be pleased with him), that the Prophet ﷺ said: *"There will be tribulations during which one who sitting is better than one who is standing, and one who standing is better than one who is walking, and one who is walking is better than one who is running. He who exposes himself to them will be drawn to them and whoever finds a refuge from them, let him seek protection therein."* Narrated by al-Bukhari (3601) and Muslim (2886).

There have been many prophecies by the Prophet Muhammad, about the last days and a great war (Armeggedon) after which the Mahdi عليهوسلم appears and Jesus عليهوسلم returns. If we find ourselves in these days, then the above hadith is applicable which scholars have interpreted to mean: "Stay in your homes, look after your family and don't get involved in the fighting".

Jihad of the Heart - The Inner Path of Struggle

A Sufi gathering in Istanbul

MODERN DAY TARIQATS OR SUFI ORDERS

There are many modern day Sufi Tariqats all around the world including the Naqshbandi, Chisti, Mevlevi, Qadiriyya to name a few. They hold gatherings, perform *dhikr* or remembrance of Allah and carry out much charitable work.

All Shar'iah Imams from the four main schools of thought advise learning from a sheikh or authorised teacher. "If you do not have a sheikh then Shaytan is your sheikh." (Imam Shafi'i) Contrary to some scholars who advise to skip having a teacher and go straight to Allah, including Salafi and Wahabi scholars, it is not possible to simply, 'go straight to Allah'. We may have an experience of Allah momentarily but in order to fully achieve closeness to Him, we must first find our guide. This is the first step of humility, to recognise there are those out there who know more than us.

There are certain criteria for a true guide, a Master of the Self, a true enlightened sheikh - they must know and follow the *Shar'iah* in all its details and not practise innovations. They must also know of the science of *Tassawuf* and the purification of the self. They must have written permission from their sheikh for guidance. They must not charge any fee. They inherit their manners from the Holy Prophet ﷺ himself and have great love and respect for the Prophet ﷺ and all of Allah's Creation. The heart feels at peace in their presence.

FINDING YOUR SHEIKH AND GUIDE

The heartfelt *du'a* or prayer of finding one's guide is a *du'a* that Allah loves to answer. May Allah grant us all *tawfiq*, success, in our journeys to Him.

"Every soul will taste death, and you will only be given your (full) compensation on the Day of Resurrection. So he who is drawn away from the Fire and admitted to Paradise has attained (his desire). And what is the life of this world except the enjoyment of delusion." (Al-Imran 3:185)

Sheikh Nazim al Haqqani, the 40th sheikh of the Naqshbandi Sufi Order

DISCIPLINING THE DONKEY

"An hour's worth of contemplation is equivalent to seventy years of worshipping." (Tafsir Ruhul Bayan, Volume 8)

In Sufi thought, the untrained ego is often compared to a donkey - stubborn and not very bright. To train our donkey we need self discipline which is the cornerstone of the path to nearness to Allah. As we impose some discipline, we soon see our donkey kick and bray. Even a tiny thing may cause a violent storm in ourselves. Inner attention requires practise and training, much like a soldier preparing for battle, we are preparing for the greater Jihad. Following the *Shar'iah*, which translated means, 'the well trodden path', is the very best training for the ego, keeping it away from disliked actions and preparing it for Divine service.

For thousands of years, mystics have taken to the mountains, removed themselves from society, practised abstinence and patience. Even though we may be disheartened at the extent of the ego's infiltration and complete take over of our system, there is help at hand.

IS THERE A BATTLE GOING ON WITHIN YOU?

Anyone who has experienced depression, anxiety or grief or suffered from cancer or other major illnesses, will agree that it seems a battle is going on. A battle for life, for wholeness and for happiness rages in our consciousness.

When a country is invaded, the leaders and civilians are protected and the military takes over. Many people who have experienced trauma find that 'the military' is often in control. The wiser inner self has been exiled and it is not until the country or system retrieves its powerful leader, who can contain and bring peace to all the warring factions, that the battles stop.

For Muslims, seeing the noble example of the Prophet ﷺ gives them the courage to be positive in the face of darkness, to stand up against sickness, the negativity of the mind and overwhelming emotions.

We have seen how great battles were won in the time of the Prophet ﷺ. The Prophet's ﷺ life and the events can be seen as a story or allegory for our own spiritual journey. The unbelievers of Makkah represent our unbelief. The Prophet ﷺ represents the perfected soul. The battles represent the internal struggles. The struggle to build a good society represents our own efforts to build up the solid foundations of good practices and to become a just and fair person.

So how in this modern day and age can we be victorious in this struggle?

The enlightened teachers recommend a practice called *taffakur,* or, contemplation. By spending time in prayer and meditation it is possible to slow the internal system down enough to witness what is going on, to discover where our internal battle lines are. We can find and then negotiate with the leaders to bring about a peaceful resolution and invite them to Islam. It is related from Abu Sa`eed al-Khudree that the Prophet ﷺ said:

"The best Jihad is a word of justice (or a word of truth) before a tyrannical king." (Tirmidhi)

This is when he alluded to the internal tyrant of the rebellious ego. Then, we can follow the practices of the Prophet ﷺ of the journeying of the heart to the Presence of the Lord ﷻ.

"The strong one is not one that overcomes people, the strong ones are they who overcome their ego." (Sheikh Hisham Kabbani)

Conclusion

Within his lifetime, the Prophet Muhammad ﷺ brought peace and social justice to a land where there was little. He dispelled darkness with the light that was brought by the Holy Qur'an and his noble example.

The Prophet ﷺ inspired such love that old habits fell away, and a new religion was born.

The Prophet ﷺ gave a perfect example for Muslims to follow: not only in personal conduct, but in his social and political policies that endure to this day, almost fifteen hundred years later.

Through Jihad of the Tongue, the Prophet ﷺ taught the religion and the Holy Qur'an.

Through Jihad of the Hand, the Prophet ﷺ established a society built on justice and equality.

Through Jihad of the Sword, he ﷺ commanded an army to fight against those set to destroy Islam, modelling correct and just actions in military conflict.

Through Jihad of the Heart, he ﷺ guided the Muslims to their Lord and to the ultimate victory: that of attaining Paradise and eternal happiness.

Over the centuries that followed, Islam spread as far as Europe and China, as the Prophet ﷺ predicted, with great civilsations flourishing with outstanding architecture, education and spiritual learning.

In Book Two, we join the the four Rightly Guided Khalifs, Abu Bakr as-Siddique ر, 'Umar al-Khattab ر, 'Uthman ibn Affan ر and 'Ali ibn abu-Talib ر, to hear about their extraodinary efforts to ensure that the principles of peace and justice took hold throughout Arabia after the 'Ummah was thrown into chaos when the Prophet ﷺ died. We will see how they achieved this incredible feat and the remarkable spread of the new religion in the first century of Islam.

The Blue Mosque in Istanbul, Turkey. Built in 1609 during Sultan Ahmed I's rule.

APPENDIX 1
HOW DO WE GATHER HISTORICAL EVIDENCE IN ISLAM?

How do we know that what we hear about someone who lived almost 1,500 years ago is true? It is essential to know where information comes from and if sources are historically accurate to be able to give a true historical account of events such a long time ago, especially the origins of an entire faith.

Some may argue, "Surely those who loved and followed the Prophet Muhammad ﷺ could have made things up? Making up a seemingly perfect man?"

Islam is unique in having the science of hadith – this is the recording and transmission of everything that the Prophet Muhammad ﷺ said and did and the authentication of them.

The Muslims themselves are not interested in fabricated or made up sayings of the Prophet Muhammad ﷺ or his Companions and will reject a fabricated saying, even if the message sounds really good and they will accept a saying even if it is not fully understood or in some way difficult. Some hadiths at different times may contradict each other but both are kept and those knowledgeable in hadith can explain the difference based on when it was said and the context.

Scholars spend many years studying these sciences and become experts in these fields. They also have to have an *ijaza* or permission to them teach to other people. There are many who study at a college who then post things on the internet and call themselves authorities but actually are not qualified to do so.

The science of hadith includes sayings by the Noble *Sahaba* (Companions) of the Prophet ﷺ. After this time and at the start of the Umayyad Empire, there are Islamic historians who wrote accounts which, along with non-Muslim historical evidence, form the basis of what we know today. And Allah knows best in all things.

In the time of the Prophet ﷺ not many people wrote things down and so the close Companions would take care to memorise as much as they could of what the Prophet ﷺ said. They knew they had the responsibility to preserve the teachings that they were so privileged to hear.

Not all of the Prophet's ﷺ close Companions transmitted hadith. This transmission of hadith required vast amount of precise memory. Some of the best narrators were Abu Hurayra who narrated 5,374 hadiths, Ibn `Umar who narrated 2,600 hadiths, 'Anas b. Malik who narrated 2,286 hadiths, `Aisha (the Prophet's ﷺ wife) – narrated 2,210 hadiths, Ibn `Abbas – narrated 1,660 hadiths, Jabir b. `Abd Allah – narrated 1,540 hadiths and Abu Sa`id al-Khudri – narrated 1,170 hadiths.

The hadith was then passed through the generations until they were formally written down. We will see in the next page about how Imam Bukhari, the most famous collector of hadith, went about ordering them.

THE HIGHEST STANDARDS OF AUTHENTICITY

Not every hadith passed down is accepted; the rules are very strict and completely depend on who narrated it. For a report to be considered authentic/sound, it must meet five conditions:

1. *Itisal as-Sanad* (A fully connected chain of narration): This means that each narrator in the chain of narration took directly from the one before him, and he in turn took the narration directly from the one before him and so on from the beginning of the sanad (chain of narration) till its end.

2. *`Adalatur-Ruwat* (Trustworthiness/reliability of the narrators): That every narrator can be described (after research) to be a Muslim, adult, free from major sins (and one who does not commit sins openly), and the narrator cannot be one who possesses bad manners and hateful habits. So the narrator should be known for taqwa and piety.

3. *Dabt ar-Ruwat* (That every narrator in the chain is precise and accurately reports what he took from the narrator before him): This can be done in two ways: a) either accurately reporting what has been memorised or, b) accurately reporting what he has written down.

4. *`Adam ash-Shudhoodh* (Absence of contradiction of that which is stronger): Meaning that the hadith cannot contradict another hadith that has been reported by narrators that are more trustworthy and greater in precision.

5. *`Adam al-`Illah* (Absence of hidden defects): This is where there maybe a subtle hidden defect that deems the hadith as being inauthentic – whilst on the surface it may seem sound.

If any one or more of these conditions is absent then the hadith cannot be considered as *saheeh* or sound.

The hadiths are then collected into voloumes, the most famous being al-Bukhari and Muslim.

Appendix II

Muhammad ibn Isma'il al-Bukhari - *The Greatest Hadith Scholar*

810-870 C.E.   194-256 A.H.

Muhammad al-Bukhari was born in Bukhara, Uzbekestan.

Al-Bukhari is the most well known compiler of hadith: 7,500 hadiths in 97 books He memorised 300,000 hadith in total over his life. It is universally acknowledged as the most authentic book after the Holy Qur'an.

When he was a child, he became blind and none of the doctors could heal him. His father had died when he was young and his mother, a widow, was very pious and prayed so much to Allah to restore her sons eyesight. Allah accepted her prayer and his eyesight was restored.

When he was ten he became very interested in hadith and studied them all the time. Even his teachers in his hadith class would sometimes get corrections from him. He had an amazing memory, and by the time he was sixteen he had memorised all of the books of `Abdullah ibn al-Mubarak, al-Waki and other learned companions of Imam Abu Hanifa ﺭ.

He then studied in Makkah and travelled to many places to gain as much knowledge as possible:

"To seek knowledge, I travelled to Egypt and Syria twice, Basra four times; spent six years at the Hijaz."

CHARACTER

Yusuf ibn Musa Maruzi states, "I was sitting in the central mosque of Basra when I heard a voice saying, 'O seeker of knowledge, Imam Muhammad ibn Isma`il has arrived. Whoever wants to receive hadith from him should present himself in his company.'" Marazi says, "I saw a thin, weak young man near the pillar who was praying salat with extreme humbleness and humility and that was Imam Bukhari. As soon as the announcement was made, curious people from all directions began to gather around."

Warraq goes on to say, "When we accompanied Imam Bukhari on a journey, he would gather us in one room and would stay by himself in a separate room. Once I saw Imam Bukhari get up between fifteen and twenty times during the night and every time, he lit the lamp with his own hands. He took some hadith out, marked them and then placed his head on his pillow and laid on his couch. I said to him, 'Why did you go through all this trouble during the night, when you could have woken me up [so that I could help you].' He replied, 'You are young and are in need of sound sleep and I did not want to disturb your sleep.'"

He was very generous with this wealth. Sometimes, he would give three thousand dirhams as a donation in one day. Warraq says that Imam Bukhari's earnings were five hundred dirhams per month and he would spend all of it on his students, most of whom were poor.

An artist's impression of al-Bukhari

REMARKABLE MEMORY

Imam Bukhari was a man with an outstanding memory. Hashid ibn Isma`il states that in his childhood, "Imam Bukhari used to go with us to the Scholars of Basra to listen to hadith. All of us used to write hadith down, except Imam Bukhari. After sixteen days, we thought about it and we condemned Imam Bukhari saying that, 'You have wasted so many days work by not writing down ahadith.' Imam Bukhari asked us to bring our notes to him. So we all brought our notes, upon which Imam Bukhari began to read hadith one by one from the top of his head until he narrated to us more than fifteen thousand! Hearing these, it seemed that Imam Bukhari was reteaching us all of the hadith we had noted."

The garden outside al-Bukhari's tomb, Uzbekestan

The entrance to the tomb of Imam Bukhari in Uzbekestan

PIETY

He was bestowed with the highest rank of piety and righteousness. He feared Allah very much inwardly and outwardly. He prevented himself from backbiting and suspicion and always respected the rights of others. Bakr ibn Munir relates that Imam Bukhari said, "I am hopeful that when I meet my Lord, He will not take account of me because I never backbited."

Imam Bukhari was so vigilant in his worship that he would pray nawafil and keep fasts in abundance. He would complete the recitation of the whole Qur'an daily in the month of Ramadan and also recited ten chapters of the Holy Qur'an deep in the night. He would complete the Holy Qur'an in the Tarawih prayers; always reciting twenty verses in each rak`at. He was very courteous, tolerant and gentle. He never became angry if mistreated by other persons and prayed for forgiveness for those who attributed evil to him. If he needed to correct any person, he would never embarrass him in public.

Al-Bukhari had a very strong connection to the Prophet Muhammad ﷺ. When he wanted to check a hadith, he would pray, then sleep. The Prophet Muhammad ﷺ would then inform him in a dream if the hadith was accurate, and where he should place the hadith in the collection.

PASSING TO THE NEXT LIFE

Imam Bukhari devoted his entire life in the search of the way of life given by the Holy Prophet ﷺ, in acting upon his sayings and researching into this science. His each and every action was a fragment of the way of the Messenger. Warraq stated: "In a dream, I once saw Imam Bukhari walking behind the Prophet ﷺ and his feet would fall exactly where the feet of the blessed Prophet ﷺ had fallen."

The Janazah prayer was performed over Imam Bukhari and his body was covered with soil. A beautiful musk smell exuded from the earth of his grave which lasted for several days. People from far and wide began to visit it in astonishment and also took handfuls of earth from his grave for blessings.

Appendix III

The Constitution of Medina

The first constitution to have ever been written in the world

The following is a translation into English of what was alleged (by Ibn Hisham in the early 800s C.E.) to have been the text of the Constitution of Medina by Muslim scholar Muhamad Hamidullah based on the following sources: the Seerah of Ibn Hisham which quotes the Seerah of Ibn Ishaq, Abu Ubaid's Kitab-al-Amwal, and Ibn Kathir's al-Bidayah wan Nihaya. A comparative translation of the two versions by Ibn Ishaq in Ibn Hisham's recension and Abu Ubaid has been published by Michael Lecker, who highlights the differences between the two texts.

A Translation of the Constitution of the City-State of Madina in the Time of the Prophet ﷺ.

In the name of God, the Beneficent and the Merciful

(1) This is a prescript of Muhammad ﷺ, the Prophet and Messenger of God (to operate) between the faithful and the followers of Islam from among the Quraysh and the people of Medina and those who may be under them, may join them and take part in wars in their company.

(2) They shall constitute a separate political unit (Ummat) as distinguished from all the people (of the world).

(3) The emigrants from the Quraysh shall be (responsible) for their own ward; and shall pay their blood-money in mutual collaboration and shall secure the release of their own prisoners by paying their ransom from themselves, so that the mutual dealings between the Believers be in accordance with the principles of goodness and justice.

(4) And Banu 'Awf shall be responsible for their own ward and shall pay their blood-money in mutual collaboration, and every group shall secure the release of its own prisoners by paying their ransom from themselves so that the dealings between the believers be in accordance with the principles of goodness and justice.

(5) And Banu al-Harith-ibn-Khazraj shall be responsible for their own ward and shall pay their blood-money in mutual collaboration and every group shall secure the release of its own prisoners by paying their ransom from themselves, so that the dealings between the believers be in accordance with the principles of goodness and justice.

(6) And Banu Sa'ida shall be responsible for their own ward, and shall pay their blood-money in mutual collaboration and every group shall secure the release of its own prisoners by paying their ransom from themselves, so that the dealings between the believers be in accordance with the principles of goodness and justice.

(7) And Banu Jusham shall be responsible for their own ward and shall pay their blood-money in mutual collaboration and every group shall secure the release of its own prisoners by paying their ransom so that the dealings between the believers be in accordance with the principles of goodness and justice.

(8) And Banu an-Najjar shall be responsible for their own ward and shall pay their blood-money in mutual collaboration and every group shall secure the release of its own prisoners by paying their ransom so that the dealings between the believers be in accordance with the principles of goodness and justice.

(9) And Banu 'Amr ibn 'Awf shall be responsible for their own ward and shall pay their blood-money in mutual collaboration and every group shall secure the release of its own prisoners by paying their ransom, so that the dealings between the believers be in accordance with the principles of goodness and justice.

(10) And Banu al-Nabit shall be responsible for their own ward and shall pay their blood-money in mutual collaboration and every group shall secure the release of its own prisoners by paying their ransom so that the dealings between the believers be in accordance with the principles of goodness and justice.

(11) And Banu al-Aws shall be responsible for their own ward and shall pay their blood-money in mutual collaboration and every group shall secure the release of its own prisoners by paying their ransom, so that the dealings between the believers be in accordance with the principles of goodness and justice.

(12) (a) And the Believers shall not leave any one, hard-pressed with debts, without affording him some relief, in order that the dealings between the believers be in accordance with the principles of goodness and justice. (b) Also no believer shall enter into a contract of clientage with one who is already in such a contract with another believer.

(13) And the hands of pious Believers shall be raised against every such person as rises in rebellion or attempts to acquire anything by force or is guilty of any sin or excess or attempts to spread mischief among the believers ; their hands shall be raised all together against such a person, even if he be a son to any one of them.

(14) A Believer will not kill a Believer [in retaliation] for a non-Believer and will not aid a non-Believer against a Believer.

(15) The protection (dhimmah) of Allah is one, the least of them [i.e., the Believers] is entitled to grant protection (yujir) that is binding for all of them. The Believers are each other's allies (mawali) to the exclusion of other people.

(16) And that those who will obey us among the Jews, will have help and equality. Neither shall they be oppressed nor will any help be given against them.

(17) And the peace of the Believers shall be one. If there be any war in the way of God, no Believer shall be under any peace (with the enemy) apart from other believers, unless it (this peace) be the same and equally binding on all.

(18) And all those detachments that will fight on our side will be relieved by turns.

(19) And the Believers as a body shall take blood vengeance in the way of God.

(20) (a) And undoubtedly pious Believers are the best and in the rightest course. (b) And that no associator (non-Muslim subject) shall give any protection to the life and property of a Qurayshite, nor shall he come in the way of any believer in this matter.

(21) And if any one intentionally murders a believer, and it is proved, he shall be killed in retaliation, unless the heir of the murdered person be satisfied with blood-money. And all Believers shall actually stand for this ordinance and nothing else shall be proper for them to do.

(22) And it shall not be lawful for any one, who has agreed to carry out the provisions laid down in this code and has affixed his faith in God and the Day of Judgment, to give help or protection to any murderer, and if he gives any help or protection to such a person, God's Curse and Wrath shall be on him on the Day of Resurrection, and no money or compensation shall be accepted from such a person.

(23) And that whenever you differ about anything, refer it to God and to Muhammad ﷺ.

(24) And the Jews shall share with the believers the expenses of war so long as they fight in conjunction,

(25) And the Jews of Banu ʻAwf shall be considered as one community (Ummat) along with the believers—for the Jews their religion, and for the Muslims theirs, be one client or patron. But whoever does wrong or commits treachery brings evil only on himself and his household.

(26) And the Jews of Banu an-Najjar shall have the same rights as the Jews of Banu ʻAwf.

(27) And the Jews of Banu al-Harith shall have the same rights as the Jews of Banu ʻAwf.

(28) And the Jews of Banu Saʻida shall have the same rights as the Jews of Banu ʻAwf

(29) And the Jews of Banu Jusham shall have the same rights as the Jews of Banu ʻAwf.

(30) And the Jews of Banu al-Aws shall have the same rights as the Jews of Banu ʻAwf.

(31) And the Jews of Banu Thaʻlaba shall have the same rights as the Jews of Banu ʻAwf. But whoever does wrong or commits treachery brings evil only on himself and his household.

(32) And Jafna, who are a branch of the Thaʼlaba tribe, shall have the same rights as the mother tribes.

(33) And Banu ash-Shutaiba shall have the same rights as the Jews of Banu ʻAwf; and they shall be faithful to, and not violators of, treaty.

(34) And the mawlas (clients) of Thaʼlaba shall have the same rights as those of the original members of it.

(35) And the sub-branches of the Jewish tribes shall have the same rights as the mother tribes.

(36) (a) And that none of them shall go out to fight as a soldier of the Muslim army, without the per-mission of Muhammad ﷺ. (b) And no obstruction shall be placed in the way of any oneʼʼs retaliation for beating or injuries; and whoever sheds blood brings it upon himself and his household, except he who has been wronged, and Allah demands the most righteous fulfillment of this [treaty].

(37) (a) And the Jews shall bear the burden of their expenses and the Muslims theirs.

(b) And if any one fights against the people of this code, their (i.e., of the Jews and Muslims) mutual help shall come into operation, and there shall be friendly counsel and sincere behaviour between them; and faithfulness and no breach of covenant.

(38) And the Jews shall be bearing their own expenses so long as they shall be fighting in conjunction with the Believers.

(39) And the Valley of Yathrib (Medina) shall be a Haram (sacred place) for the people of this code.

(40) The clients (mawla) shall have the same treatment as the original persons (i.e., persons accepting clientage). He shall neither be harmed nor shall he himself break the covenant.

(41) And no refuge shall be given to any one without the permission of the people of the place (i.e., the refugee shall have no right of giving refuge to others).

(42) And that if any murder or quarrel takes place among the people of this code, from which any trouble may be feared, it shall be referred to God and Godʼʼs Messenger, Muhammad ﷺ; and God will be with him who will be most particular about what is written in this code and act on it most faithfully.

(43) The Quraysh shall be given no protection nor shall they who help them.

(44) And they (i.e., Jews and Muslims) shall have each other's help in the event of any one invading Yathrib.

(45) (a) And if they (i.e., the Jews) are invited to any peace, they also shall offer peace and shall be a party to it; and if they invite the believers to some such affairs, it shall be their (Muslims) duty as well to reciprocate the dealings, excepting that any one makes a religious war. (b) On every group shall rest the responsibility of (repulsing) the enemy from the place which faces its part of the city.

(46) And the Jews of the tribe of al-Aws, clients as well as original members, shall have the same rights as the people of this code: and shall behave sincerely and faithfully towards the latter, not perpetrating any breach of covenant. As one shall sow so shall he reap. And God is with him who will most sincerely and faithfully carry out the provisions of this code.

(47) And this prescript shall not be of any avail to any oppressor or breaker of covenant. And one shall have security whether one goes out to a campaign or remains in Medina, or else it will be an oppression and breach of covenant. And God is the Protector of him who performs the obligations with faithfulness and care, as also His Messenger Muhammad ﷺ.

The interior corridors at the Hassan II Mosque in Casablanca, Morocco.

ACKNOWLEDGEMENTS

This book was inspired by the work of Sheikh Hisham Kabbani, especially his book entitled, 'Jihad - Principles in Leadership in War and Peace'. I would also like to thank Hana Horack-Elyafi, Ajsa Gutic and Rose McBride for editing.

May Allah accept this humble attempt and forgive any errors or mistakes.

REFERENCES

The Messenger of Allah by Hajja Amina Adil, published by The Islamic Supreme Council of America, 2002

Battles by the Prophet, in the Light of the Qur'an by Sayyid Ammenul Hasan Rizvi, published by S. Abdul Majeed & Co., Malaysia, 1997

Jihad by Sheikh Hisham Kabbani, published by The Islamic Supreme Council of America 2010

Sahih al-Bukhari, published by Darussalam, Saudi Arabia, 1997

Muhammad Messenger of Allah Ash-Shifa of Qadi 'Iyad, translated by Aisha Abdurrahman Bewley, Medina Press 1991

Men Around the Messenger by Khalid Muhammad Khalid, Al-Manara Press

The Islamic History Podcast - https://islamichistorypodcast.com

https://lci.org.uk/courses/snapshot-from-madinah-the-structure-of-the-prophetic-society/ by Sheikh Ahmed Saad al-Azhari

http://1000gooddeeds.com/2012/11/20/10-islamic-rules-of-war/

http://ilmfeed.com/8-rules-of-engagement-taught-by-the-prophet-muhammad/

https://islamqa.org/hanafi/qibla-hanafi/42543 - Sh Gibrael

http://islamicsupremecouncil.org/understanding-islam/legal-rulings/5-jihad-a-misunderstood-concept-from-islam.html?start=10

http://eshaykh.com/hadith/companion-narrators-ranking-by-numbers/

http://lostislamichistory.com/jerusalem-and-umar-ibn-al-khattab/

https://aasims.wordpress.com/tag/chronology-of-events-in-the-life-of-muhammad-pbuh/

http://www.iupui.edu/~msaiupui/qaradawistatus.html

http://legendaryleeph.blogspot.com/2016/03/the-life-of-khalid-ibn-walid-ra-sword.html

https://sunnah.com/

https://www.islamicfinder.org/knowledge/biography/story-of-imam-bukhari/

https://yaqeeninstitute.org/mohammad-elshinawy/how-the-prophet-muhammad-rose-above-enmity-and-insult/

https://mkshafiisblog.wordpress.com/2019/04/16/great-warriors-of-islam-khawlah-bint-al-azwar-the-warrior-woman/

https://www.islamweb.net/en/article/157807/the-battle-of-mutah

https://www.bl.uk/sacred-texts/articles/sufism

https://www.wikipedia.org

https://www.bbc.com/culture/article/20191014-abdus-salam-the-muslim-science-genius-forgotten-by-history

https://www.nbcnews.com/news/world/muslims-give-more-charity-others-uk-poll-says-flna6c10703224

https://www.theguardian.com/social-enterprise-network/2013/mar/13/best-bits-islamic-finance-ethical-capitalism

Images

Cover illustration by Hana Horack-Elyafi

Illustrations in the Battles of the Prophet stories by Hana Horack-Elyafi

Cover design and layout by Yasmin Watson

Other images from Wikicommons

Adobe Stock Photos & Images

HONOURIFICS

Traditionally in Islam, phrases of respect are added after mentioning Allah ﷻ, the Prophet Muhammad ﷺ, the other prophets, the Prophet's ﷺ Companions and the Saints.

ﷻ	*Jalla jalaluhu*: "May his Glory be glorified."
ﷺ	*Sallahu 'alayhi wa sallam*: "Peace and blessing be upon him.
عليهوسلم	*'Alayhi sallam*: "Peace be upon them."
ر	*Radhiya llahu 'anhu*: "Well-pleased is Allah with them."
ق	*Qaddas-Allahu sirrah*: "May God sanctify their secret."

Editorial note:
I have decided, for the purpose of this book, to capitalise "Jihad" throughout. I would like to point out that this is not the standard method, it would normally be considered a common noun and written, "jihad".

INDEX

Other Books by Halima Publishing!

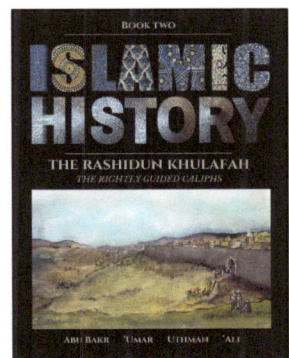

The second book in the series of Young Person's Guide to Islamic History. Focusing on the fascinating histories of the four Rightly Guided Khulafah; Sayyidina Abu Bakr As-Siddique, Sayyidina 'Umar ibn Khattab, Sayyidina 'Uthman and Sayyidina 'Ali ibn Abi Talib. For children 10+

ISBN 978-1-999802738

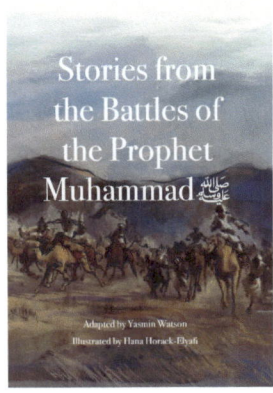

This exciting adaptation of the famous battles of early Islam follows the experiences of a fictional character, Abdul Karim, as he joins the Prophet Muhammad ﷺ in battle. Based on original sources. For children 8+

ISBN 979-8-8392260-8-1

In this book, children and young people can find out miraculous links with the Holy Qur'an and modern day science. With Montessori inspired science activities to do at home. For children 7+

ISBN 978-1-9998027-0-7

www.ingramcontent.com/pod-product-compliance
Lightning Source LLC
Chambersburg PA
CBHW041549120626

46551CB00002B/158